WELDED

Forming Racial Bonds That Last

Derrick Hawkins & Jay Stewart

iDisciple®

ISBN: 978-1734952223

Printed in China

Published by Giving Publishing, 2555 Northwinds Parkway, Alpharetta GA 30009.

WELDED

FORMING RACIAL BONDS THAT LAST

CONTENTS

6

DEDICATION

7

SHOUT-OUTS

19

CHAPTER 1
A CHANCE MEETING

27

CHAPTER 2
A BETTER
NARRATIVE

59

CHAPTER 5
WE ARE BETTER
TOGETHER

67

CHAPTER 6
PIECES/PĒS

105

CHAPTER 9
STRUGGLES

123

CHAPTER 10
SHAPING CULTURE

12
FOREWORD

15
PREFACE

37
CHAPTER 3
THE PRIORITY
OF JESUS

45
CHAPTER 4
UNSUNG HEROES

79
CHAPTER 7
WHAT NOW?

91
CHAPTER 8
BARRIERS

143
ABOUT THE
AUTHORS

144
ACKNOWLEDGMENTS

DEDICATION

We dedicate

"WELDED"

to our wives

MELANIE STEWART
&
ROSHONDA HAWKINS,

two of the most compassionate and
courageous people we know.

SHOUT-OUTS

"With the ongoing racial tensions in our nation, many are feeling hopeless and without an answer. That's why I'm so thankful for this very timely and candid book by Jay Stewart and Derrick Hawkins. *Welded: Forming Racial Bonds That Last* leads us to the answer so many are desperately seeking. Written from two unique perspectives, this book gives us a better understanding of how we can celebrate our differences, cultivate better relationships, and move forward together in unity."

Robert Morris
Founding Lead Senior Pastor, Gateway Church
Bestselling Author of *The Blessed Life*, *Beyond Blessed*, and *Take the Day Off*

"The gospel is full of encounters to illustrate God's character and purpose. What God has done in the story of the book *Welded* to unite pastors Derrick Hawkins and Jay Stewart at The Refuge is a beautiful representation of the gospel. One from a predominantly black church. One from a predominantly white church. Both joined together, united in the gospel to help heal a city torn apart by racial injustice after a tragic police shooting. We may be a nation that is divided, but *Welded* shows how the gospel unites us to become more like Jesus. ***Welded* is a much-needed story to inspire the Church to understand racial reconciliation and be guided on what to do about it.** I look forward to seeing how God will continue to work in their story."

Dr. Tony Evans
Senior pastor of Oak Cliff Bible Fellowship and bestselling author of *Kingdom Man* and *The Tony Evans Study Bible* and Bible Commentary.

"Welded—Forming Racial Bonds That Last challenges us to lay aside our preferences, biases, prejudices and assumptions and celebrate the image of God in every human being. Convicting as well as encouraging, this book is for every believer who wants to see racial reconciliation become a reality in our generation."

Samuel Rodriguez
New Season Lead Pastor
NHCLC President
Author of *"You Are Next!"*
Executive Producer *Breakthrough* The Movie

"We have known Pastors Jay and Derrick for many years and have witnessed how the gospel has transformed them and God has used their story to impact their community. In *Welded,* they show courageous leadership and reveal what can happen when true friendship bonds together to heal a divided city. The Refuge 'welding' together as one church is an example that can inspire us all to be united in Christ. Our nation needs more leaders like Jay and Derrick to take a stand against division and point people to Jesus, the ultimate healer."

David and Jason Benham
Expert Ownership entrepreneurs and bestselling authors
of *Whatever the Cost* and *Living Among Lions*

"Pastor Jay Stewart has been an important voice in my life for more than two decades now. The story of reconciliation and unity that Jay and Derrick share throughout the pages of *Welded* causes hope to rise. Their experiences carry wisdom that is guaranteed to both challenge and inspire."

Mike Weaver
Lead singer of *Big Daddy Weave*, award-winning songwriter of *"Redeemed"* and *"Audience of One"*

"I firmly believe that God divinely connected Jay Stewart and Derrick Hawkins for such a time as this. The earth is in trouble and there is so much racial division, but God knew that we would need to see Him at this time. *Welded* gives us a clear picture of God crossing barriers to show Himself to the world in the lives of two great men. This is God!"

John F. Hannah
Senior Pastor of New Life Southeast in Chicago
Author and international speaker

"Welded: Forming Racial Bonds That Last is a beautiful story of how unity can be found in the celebration of diversity. Our friend Jay Stewart has co-authored a relevant message that promotes faith, hope, and love while championing racial reconciliation."

John & Lisa Bevere
Best-selling Authors and Ministers
Co-founders of *Messenger International*

"We are living in dark, divided times. For people who want to believe in the promise of this nation, that we are more good than bad, more united than divided, there are few sources of hope. Pastor Derrick and Pastor Jay's story is one. The tale of their friendship, their partnership, their joint leadership, and their refusal to accept anything less than the kingdom of heaven on earth, is a beacon of light for a nation that's hurting, illuminating a path through the dim tunnel of our division. Their story will haunt you. It will inspire you. It will change your perspective, and maybe even your life."

Batya Ungar-Sargon
Opinion editor of *"The Forward"*

Welded is a must read! The message will resonate in your heart and mind. This powerful book serves as both an inspiration and a playbook for churches, communities, and businesses to build bridges and to knock down walls of division. You will be provoked and challenged by its content! Start welding!

Dr. Choco DeJesus
2013 Time Magazine Top 100 Most Influential People
Author of *In the Gap* and *Move Into More*
General Treasurer of the Assemblies of God

"In a culture of division, Jay and Derrick shepherd us towards the better way. Their story is compelling; their testimony is a call to the Church to rise above our racial challenges. *Welded* is a gift to the believer who longs to honor the heart of God. I'm grateful to know these men and bear witness to their bond."

Lisa Whittle
Bestselling Author, Podcast Host of the *Jesus Over Everything Show*, Bible Teacher

"We are living in one of the most racially divided climates this nation has seen in recent memory. Darkness has used racism as one of the most powerful weapons to provoke fear and the hatred of others in these times of conflict and economic uncertainties. Very seldom are miracles of true unity in diversity brought to the forefront. *Welded* provides a needed narrative that MUST be told."

Will Ford
Co-founder of The Dream Stream Company, Author of *The Dream King—How the Dream of Martin Luther King, Jr. is Being Fulfilled to Heal Racism in America*

"Our great friends Jay Stewart and Derrick Hawkins are SIGNS of what God can do when we follow His heart. This powerful book weaves together profound insights, scriptural truths, and their incredible and profound story. We are convinced that this book holds the key to the future of America and the subsequent generations. Their story is so powerful, authentic, and Kingdom-centered in a way that inspires hope and provides a refresher on the value of racial unity, walking in love, and the appreciation of diversity. This is not only a MUST READ, but it should be shared with as many people as possible. We highly recommend *Welded*."

Sean and Christa Smith
Authors/Evangelists, Point Blank Ministries

"Pastor Jay Stewart has been a leading voice to pastors for many years. *Welded: Forming Racial Bonds That Last* is an amazing story and true account of Pastor Jay's godly leadership to people in the church. I am thankful for this book and my personal friendship with Pastor Jay. His leadership has made a positive impact on my life and the church I pastor."

Matthew Barnett, New York Times Bestselling Author & Founder of the Dream Center

FOREWORD

What does it mean to be unified? Does it mean agreement? Does it mean cooperation? Does it mean harmony? It could mean all of those things one way or another. But at the core of unity, I believe, is the word "intention."

So much of being unified is dependent upon one's intent. Another way to say it is, Do you want to? Do we want to be unified?

As we look around our world today, we see division everywhere. Especially in the U.S. and in the realms of religion, politics, and race. What's ironic to me about most of the division we see is that if you asked each sector if they "wanted" the division to be present, most would say no. Yet, still the division exists. Why?

Intention. I would venture to say that most who say they want unity probably want something else and something more.

Unity is often overcome by a greater desire. When the desire shifts, intention goes along with it.

- Economics or generosity.
- Freedom or protection.
- Peace of mind or accomplishment.
- Grace or Truth.
- Love or power.

No matter how you spin it, something always overrides unity—forcing us back into our silos and further into our clubs.

But unity in spite of the differences seeks to rise above the fray in order to fight for connection. The desire to be one wins over the desire to be right. At the end of the day, intention becomes the driving force that has the ability to change the day.

FOREWORD

Jay and Derrick are the living manifestation of proper intention leading to revolutionary outcome. They have found through their efforts a way forward that many of us living in America, no matter our color, can embrace as a foundation for systemic and gospel-centric change.

If you've been praying, hoping, and screaming for a brighter day in America racially, carve out some hours and some days to read this book. Study the pages, notice the construct of the relationship and witness the true intention. In it I believe you will find the solutions you've been searching for.

—Sam Collier,
International Speaker and Author of *A Greater Story*

PREFACE

PREFACE

I had never been scuba diving but was always intrigued by the idea. I was in my early twenties and was part of a team of men constructing a church building in Jamaica, and when one of the guys suggested we go scuba diving on our free day, I jumped at the chance. I did mention to him that I was not certified and had never been, and he replied, "I can teach you what you need to know." (Yeah, I know what you are thinking. Obviously, I wasn't!)

We found a leathery-skinned Jamaican man on the beach with a gray beard, who looked like he had walked out of the pages of *Gulliver's Travels,* and he said he would rent us the equipment. My friend proceeded to give me a crash course in scuba diving right there on the beach, then we loaded our equipment into a small skiff with an outboard motor and headed to a coral reef teeming with colorful coral and brightly hued sea life. The plan was to descend to the bottom of the ocean some forty feet below and observe the breathtaking sights for forty-five minutes.

We suited up, seated ourselves on the edge of the skiff, and tumbled over backwards into the crystal-clear waters of the Caribbean. The only sound heard against the deafening silence of the ocean's abyss was that of my own breathing in the regulator. We slowly began our descent into a world of aquatic beauty, an entire universe of sorts hidden beneath the ocean's surface that makes up seventy percent of planet earth.

After only a few minutes of exploring the reef some forty feet down, my mask began leaking water. *It's all good,* I thought. *We covered this on the beach.* I tipped my head back, pulled the bottom of the mask away from my face, and exhaled air upward to release bubbles into the mask to force the water out. But as I repositioned the mask and attempted to fill my lungs with air from the tank, I had difficulty taking in a breath. My mind had already been wrestling with this concept of breathing underwater, something I had been taught for over twenty years that you were never to do! When I was finally able to inhale, I began to hyperventilate. I quickly realized I was in trouble. My friend was close by and saw a look of terror on my face. He grabbed my hands and guided me in a slow ascent back to the top.

Once I broke through the water's surface, my first instinct was to rip everything off my face in order to breathe "normal" air. But I failed to remember that strapped to my waist was a thing called a weight belt intended to keep you below the surface. My first big gulp of air was not air, but what felt like a gallon of sea water. The old Jamaican man was standing up in the skiff yelling at the top of his lungs, "KEEP DE REGULATOR IN YO MOUF! KEEP DE REGULATOR IN YO MOUF!" I nearly drowned, but somehow managed to get to the boat, and with his help I tumbled in a heap into the bottom of it, exhausted and gasping for air like a beached tuna.

The story Derrick and I lived is special and unique. It is fitting that it is shared via the pages of this book against the backdrop of a unique and unprecedented time in history. Our confused, chaotic, angry, divided world is rife with a pandemic, protests, anarchy, rioting, senseless murders, and racial dissension, leaving many people feeling as if they have been plunged into an abyss of the unknown, struggling to breathe and gasping for air. We do not claim to be the experts on how to fix things. But the beautiful struggle of our story represents hope and healing.

Author George Orwell, in his book *1984*, which was published in June of 1949, penned these words: "'It is impossible to found a civilization on fear and hatred and cruelty. It would never endure.'

'Why not?'

'It would have no vitality. It would disintegrate. It would commit suicide.'"[1]

Our nation finds itself on a slippery slope of fear and hatred, spiraling downward towards the disintegration of integrity, morals, character, and human decency, hoping for real air to breathe and something that resembles an anchor of stability. That is why we wanted to invite you into our story, the unlikely story of a middle-aged white man raised in the Deep South in Georgia in the sixties, and a street-tough, thirty-something black man raised in small town North Carolina, who both decided things could, and should, be different.

We do not think that our story can solve it all. But our desire is that it will lead you to a place where the weight belt of worry, fear, and anxiety is removed, and your lungs are once again filled with the life-giving oxygen of faith, hope, and love. Enjoy!

---

1   George Orwell, *1984* (New York: Harcourt, 1949), 257.

CHAPTER 1

1

A CHANCE MEETING

Growing up in Columbus, Georgia, my most frequent interactions with African Americans as a young boy were with two people. Alexander, whom I loved, was the janitor at my church. Since my Dad worked at the church, I saw him every week. Kind, consistently slow-moving, he had a propensity towards alcohol and on occasion was known to "borrow" a bottle or two of vanilla extract from the church's kitchen if he didn't have money for a bottle of the real stuff. And then there was Doris. I grew up in a lower-middle-class family in a two-bedroom house on 13th Avenue. My Mom worked full-time for a soft drink bottling company, and my Dad had transitioned from the world of pharmaceuticals to full-time vocational ministry when I was five. From the time I can remember, Doris stayed with us from eight to five, Monday through Friday. She fed my brother and me, whipped us whenever we needed it, got us dressed in the mornings, tracked us down in the neighborhood if we were gone too long, and to me felt like a part of our family.

Things soon changed, however, and I found myself having daily interactions with many African Americans. I boarded the yellow school bus as an anxious nine-year-old in the fall of 1972 for the trip across town to begin my third-grade school year at St. Elmo Elementary. Britt David

Elementary was much closer to my home in Georgia, but now I, along with millions of others around the country, was being introduced to the concept of forced integration.

Mind you, growing up in the Deep South in the sixties and seventies certainly had its challenges for a young, developing mind. I heard far too many people use the "N" word or tell disparaging jokes that were racially tainted. And there were certainly challenges I faced that fall day in 1972 as I stepped onto the property of St. Elmo. There were guys like Stanley. He had on a silk shirt with the top three buttons unbuttoned, hot pink pants, and platform shoes. As we stood in line outside the classroom waiting to go into Ms. Prator's class, Stanley proceeded to go from person to person asking them in a threatening manner if they knew how to kiss. He would then proceed to graphically describe a French kiss to a group of third graders who only associated kissing with "cooties" or family members.

I learned to love and accept people regardless of the color of their skin. I played sports throughout my middle and high school years and developed great friendships with African American teammates and classmates like Mark, Quincy, Andre, Mary, John, the twins Maurine and Laurine, Mattie, and Charles. As I matured in my relationship with Christ and grew in age, I saw hearts and souls much more than I did skin pigmentation.

FAST-FORWARD

My wife Melanie and I, along with a handful of people, started a new church on April 4, 2004, in a basement in a bedroom community of Charlotte, North Carolina. We knew God had called us to return to the Charlotte region and do something that we never envisioned ourselves doing. We loved the idea of church planting—as long as it was someone else doing the planting. We were willing to support them, cheer them on, and help in any way we could. But now that God had tapped us on the shoulder and made it crystal clear that we were moving from the bleachers to the playing field, it was a different ball game. The only things we really had were a clear confirmation from the Lord, a vision, and a donated sound system from Big Daddy Weave. Mike Weaver's generosity in 2004 helped set the foundation for a new church called The Refuge.

Our beginnings were humble, to say the least. We had no money, no computers, no building, no demographic studies, no billboards, no fancy intelligent LEDs, and no ARC (Association of Related Churches). For the record, I love ARC, but they were barely getting started in 2004 and were still refining the process of helping pastors plant churches. It still makes no sense to me why Scott and Sheree, Nathan and Tamsey, and Mark and Bridget left their homes in Georgia and Alabama to come be a part of this with the promise of nothing. I will forever be grateful.

That first service saw a total of about eighty people, including the kids in the "nursery," which was the two-car garage of the house we were meeting in, come together and rally around a vision of building a church that would look like heaven in its demographics and sound like heaven in its worship. We wanted to "be" the church and not just "do" church, touching our community in such a way that if we closed our doors for any reason, the community would notice and we would be missed. God breathed on those humble beginnings, despite the many things we did wrong, and over the next nine months we saw the church grow from the original forty to over four hundred. Our outreaches flourished as we served our city, people continued to come, and before long we added a second service. In only a few years' time, we grew from one weekend service to four, and from one campus to three. On our literal ten-year anniversary, we moved into and dedicated our new state-of-the-art campus that was situated on thirty acres of prime property. Then things really began to get interesting!

AN UNEXPECTED INTRODUCTION

Just two months after moving into our new building, I was approached by a stranger on a Sunday morning after our second service. A tall, young African American man introduced himself as Pastor Derrick Hawkins. He quickly shared with me that he had been asked by the founding pastors to take over as senior pastor of a church in Greensboro, North Carolina. It would involve a two-year transition, and he asked if he could meet with me for the purpose of coaching and mentoring him in preparation for that role. I told him that I loved meeting with and helping pastors, and that I would be glad to do so after I returned from a sabbatical. The backstory of the way this unexpected introduction came about is quite compelling, and somewhat funny. I'll let Derrick tell the story.

FROM DERRICK

God has a sense of humor. I remember that morning as though it were yesterday. My wife asked me to take our daughter to her hair appointment. In all honesty, I had no intention of moving from the comfort of my very cushy couch that day. However, I realized that my "yes" or "no" could very well change the direction of the day. Every husband knows the saying "happy wife, happy life." Who would have expected that one fatherly duty would turn into one of the most destiny-defining moments of my life.

As I was driving to the appointment in Salisbury, North Carolina, my car rounded the corner, where a large billboard was seemingly staring me in the face, and it grabbed my complete attention. The billboard had the name of a church, The Refuge, along with a website. I have no idea how I could've missed this massive sign for months. Almost immediately, I completely forgot how disgruntled I was over having to take my daughter to the hairstylist. I was attracted to and intrigued by the details on this sign. I pulled out my phone, started taking pictures, wrote down the information, and made my way back home to begin doing some research.

When I arrived, I told my wife what I had just experienced. I sat down in my chair and looked up the information I'd written down. I called the number posted, the phone rang, and the receptionist picked up. But something strange happened. The number I called didn't lead me to a church in Salisbury. It directed me to a church in the Concord/Kannapolis area outside of Charlotte. I had no idea that The Refuge was in the middle of opening the doors of its brand-new campus in Kannapolis. The first service had not even been held at this point. I was still struggling to understand why I was talking to someone in Concord/Kannapolis instead of Salisbury until I finally realized that this was the location of the central campus.

I remember asking the receptionist who was in charge of their graphic design work. She then transferred me to The Refuge's creative department, and I was able to speak to the imaging director. Although he was extremely busy with the demands of a growing church and a soon-to-open new campus, he invited me to come down and meet with him about potentially doing some graphic art for my church, which ironically was named The House of Refuge. Looking back in retrospect, it wasn't irony at all. It was the hand of God.

As soon as I pulled onto the grounds of The Refuge, I knew there was something different about this place. I could feel the presence of God illuminating throughout the campus. Every aspect of the church was done with such great detail and precision, from the floors to the bookstore and even the furniture selection. Everything oozed with excellence.

As we sat together in the Mug Shot, the church's coffee shop, to discuss the details of designing a sign for my church, I quickly gathered that there was a bigger picture unfolding. The imaging director, Marcello, who was from Brazil, began to talk about his encounters with God there and how his life had been deeply impacted by Pastor Jay Stewart. We talked less about the intended subject I initially came to discuss, which was graphic design, and more about The Refuge. He shared with me that Pastor Jay was an apostolic father and that he felt as though there was something I needed from him.

On the drive home, I had a strong sense that God was up to something. A few weeks later, I attended a Sunday service and heard a powerful message on revival from guest speaker Banning Liebscher. I drove home in tears, unable to stop crying. I could feel the presence of God so strongly in my car. The amazing love of God surrounded me, and I felt every ounce of it.

I left The Refuge that day knowing that it wasn't just about a sign or the simple, obedient response to my wife in taking my daughter to her hair appointment. It was a divine setup from God that would later alter my life in ways that I never would have thought possible. It would be the answer to many years of prayer, after a life filled with many disappointments. Who knew that a billboard and a chance meeting would change it all?

FROM JAY

From the first time I met with Derrick, I sensed that there was an unusual connection. I liked him from the start and was impressed by what I saw in him and by the things I heard him say. This would be the first of many meetings as we began to connect each month. And each time I grew to love and appreciate him more.

Not many months into our meeting together, the founding pastors of his church asked if they could come and meet the man pouring into their spiritual son. I'll never forget the first time I met Bishop and Pastor Allen.

They entered my office and sat down, and for the next hour or so I don't think Bishop Allen spoke more than twenty words. Not so with his wife, Pastor Allen. I surmised within the first five minutes that I would never have to wonder what was on her mind. And I loved it—and loved them— and thus began an amazing relationship of love, trust, and mutual respect. I knew I was under the microscope of scrutiny that first meeting, but apparently I checked out okay.

I do not know if I can adequately describe what God did in our relationship over the next year. We continued to meet regularly, and at times ten or twelve of their leaders would join us as I helped them prepare for the upcoming transition of leadership in their church. Oh, did I mention the name of their church? The House of Refuge. I thought it was interesting when I first learned of this, but really thought nothing more of it other than that it was cool that the names of our churches were so similar. I was asked to speak at a leadership retreat for their church, giving me the opportunity to get to know more of the great people making up this special place. Our love for one another continued to grow in an almost supernatural way. These people literally felt like family! But none of us could have predicted the incredible plan God was unfolding, and we certainly did not anticipate what would soon happen.

CHAPTER 2

CHAPTER

2

A BETTER NARRATIVE

For many years Americans were treated to a daily radio show featuring the smooth baritone voice and jaw-dropping stories of Paul Harvey. He would eloquently invite the listener into a compelling story of someone's life or of some event and then deliver his infamous line, "and now . . . the rest of the story." God began writing the story of two churches coming together in the midst of racial discord long before it actually happened. The orchestration of events in Derrick's life years prior is a picture of the ability God has to make beauty out of ashes and to cause all things to work together for the good of those who love Him and are called according to His purpose (see Romans 8:28).

DERRICK'S TESTIMONY

I was born November 28, 1983, to Michael Bost and Melanie Hawkins in the small city of Salisbury, North Carolina. Salisbury is a city with a population of about 33,000 people. My father was in the military, where he spent most of his tour in Korea. My mother dropped out of high school at a tender age after becoming pregnant with me, her first child of what would soon be four. As a result, I was raised in the home of my grandparents, Betty and Charlie McNeely.

Up until the age of thirteen, I spent most of my years with my grandmother Betty and great-grandmother Anna. At the ages of five and six, contrary to our desire, my sister and I were separated. A relative of the family adopted her, and my grandmother chose to keep me. My grandmother Betty spent most of her years working in factories and raising children. She was already raising nine children before adding me, the tenth, to the equation. My great-grandmother helped raise us as well. When we were young, we would spend most of our days at her home. Great-grandmother Anna worked year after year for the Rufty family (one of the most influential Caucasian families in her community during those times). In all those years of hard work, she never once complained about her position in life. She took every opportunity to teach me about servanthood and prayer.

I remember as a young boy Great-grandmother Anna prophesying over me that the Lord would use me to preach the gospel. Her reasoning was insightful, and some would say spot-on. She said it was because I had a head like a preacher and I liked fried chicken! I am still a lover of a good hearty serving of fried chicken to this day. My Anna died at the accomplished age of 105. She was and will always be one of the most profound influences on my life and on my faith. Great-grandmother Anna was one the wisest people I have ever known.

One of the fondest, most memorable moments of my life transpired in the small town of Mocksville, North Carolina. Mocksville was what my good friend Marty Dyson would call God's country. It was much smaller than Salisbury, if you can imagine that, and mostly filled with farmland, old barns, and fields. We moved there when I was about four years old. I remember around the age of nine playing church in the back room of our house. One particular morning, I put on my aunt's high school graduation robe. With my newly transformed preacher's robe on, I was ready to preach and lay hands on every soul I came in contact with. I was pretty sure my cousins were filled with something that day, I just wasn't sure what!

Although we often played this church game, something seemed and felt different this particular day. I felt something that I had never felt before. The presence of God overtook me, and I knew and believed that the hand of God rested upon my life. It was then that I knew I could no longer afford to play with God's Spirit. I started crying and ran to my grandmother. She asked what was wrong, but I could not tell her that I had been playing church all morning. I knew how she felt about mocking or mishandling the divine, and that she would likely have retrieved the largest switch she could find and put it to use. I made up a story about missing my mom, which she believed. From that day forward, I vowed never to play church again or to treat God's presence with anything less than great fear and respect.

Mocksville was known for being a city with a great deal of racial tension. One afternoon, while getting off the school bus, I vividly remember a truck full of men riding by. They began yelling racial slurs and shooting their guns. I ran as fast as I could for what seemed like forever until my grandmother grabbed me in her arms and held me, thanking Jesus I was alive. That was one of my earliest experiences with the ugly monster of racism, but it would not be my last.

Growing up, we never talked much about race, but there was always a clear, unspoken truth. African Americans went to their own churches while Caucasians went to theirs. Like most African Americans in the area, I went to a very traditional Baptist church. The deacons smoked, the church mothers wore great big hats, and the pastor preached messages that had the ability to put you in the deepest sleep ever. It was church business as usual until I turned eleven.

In 1994, on a Sunday morning, I made the conscious decision to go down to the altar and give my life to Christ. I felt that same feeling I felt when I was nine—the strong presence of God's hand on my life. The difference this time was that I was no longer afraid. From that moment on, I served and assisted in every way I could. My grandmothers had instilled in me from the time I was a young child the importance of serving and of having a relationship with God.

The years to follow are what I would call the dark years. One Sunday, after leaving church, I returned home and my grandfather was waiting for me with some news. He told me that I had to leave his house and move out. That morning I had made the mistake of leaving the iron on while ironing my church clothes. My grandfather decided that he had had just about all he could take. The place I had called home for as long as I could remember would no longer be that for me. It was one of the hardest days of my life. I had lived with my grandmother since I was born, and she was all I knew. I remember her looking into my tear-filled eyes and saying that I had to move in with my father. I went to my room, packed all my clothes, and with tears rolling down my face, I knew life as I had known it was over.

My dad had always been in my life. I would spend most weekends at his house. But the environment surrounding my father was entirely different from what I had become accustomed to. My dad went to church sometimes, but nowhere near as frequently as I was used to. For my father, a good time was drinking and attending cookouts. Over time, I began drifting further away from what I knew and closer to what surrounded me day in and day out.

To make matters worse, I was not always in the safest circumstances while living with my dad. For example, on one occasion a family function turned into a hostage situation. My family was robbed at gunpoint and held captive until my dad could talk to the culprits, urging them to let us go. That event shook me up, and I soon started rebelling against God. My whole world began to crumble. Betty was more than my grandmother. She was the nurturing source in my life; one that all children need. Being separated from her took a huge toll. I began smoking and hanging out with the wrong crowd in an attempt to cover up my depression and low self-esteem. I would still attend church on occasion, but by this time I was far from God, slipping further and further away as time progressed.

By the time I was eighteen, I barely attended school. I managed to graduate with my class, but I was spiritually bound, depressed, and struggling. In the summer of 2003, I learned that I had a child on the way, out of wedlock. A few months later, on August 22, my son was born stillborn. For fourteen hours I sat and stared at my lifeless son. I felt as though I was watching a smaller version of myself. It was in that moment that I heard the voice of God for the first time in four years. As clear as day, I heard Him say, "If you do not come to Me, the next death will be your own." Those words shook me to my core. Night after night for weeks I would have visitations from God. His message remained the same.

In the fall of 2004, my relationship with the young lady ended, launching me into a deeper depression. I had a high school diploma and acceptance into St. Augustine's College, but I was at the lowest point of my life. I couldn't see it, but God was still behind the scenes, ordering my steps. Unbeknownst to me, He was setting me up to have an encounter that would forever alter the direction of my life.

Shortly after arriving at St. Augustine, I met a young lady who invited me to a church service. I felt drawn to the idea of going because I had just been robbed at gunpoint for the second time in a few months. I knew this was God trying to get my attention, and I knew it was time to make a change. I went to service that evening, and for the first time in a long time, I felt the conviction of the Holy Spirit once again. After the service, she shared with me some of the most profound things I had ever heard. She told me that I was called to preach. She told me that I would connect with a woman who would then lead me to a middle-aged Caucasian gentleman while I was at my lowest. She proceeded to tell me about the apostolic call of God on my life. She continued by telling me about two ages that would be very significant for me: twenty-three and thirty. I came home after that life-changing encounter telling everyone I knew about Jesus. Everyone with whom I crossed paths was subject to hear all I had to say about the One who changed my life. I began to find my footing in the faith again, and the events that would follow in the summer would truly seal my destiny.

On August 13, 2004, around the time I was supposed to return to college for my sophomore year, I was invited to another service. This invitation was to a church back in my hometown of Salisbury. At the end of his message, the preacher gave an altar call. Something powerful came over me, and those who were there still tell the story. I responded to the altar call and completely surrendered my life to Christ. As soon as I surrendered, signs and wonders began to take place. The next morning, I woke up having visions that I could not contain or describe. I was experiencing God in a way I never had before. I was both frightened and anxious to understand what was happening to me. I saw visions of things that are still coming to pass to this day, but the lines were blurred between what I saw spiritually and what was actually occurring naturally.

I wandered off and was later located in Kings Mountain, North Carolina. I could not recall how I got there, nor could I recollect what happened in the time between getting lost and being found. My father and friends came to pick me up, worried and distraught about how this could have even happened. There was a profound spiritual battle taking place, and this was the first time I had ever experienced demonic activity and spiritual warfare on that level.

I was literally in warfare for the next ten days, and because of this warfare, I was committed to an insane asylum. Yes, you read it correctly. I was misunderstood. I didn't understand, and the people around me were not spiritually mature enough to understand all that was taking place. For the next ten days, I had visions about the Kingdom of God. After my release, I went on to live life as usual until every prophecy the young lady had given me manifested and became reality. I met a woman by the name of Pastor Darlene Allen, and she pastored me at The House of Refuge for the next five years. It all brought me to a sign that would lead me to a middle-aged man by the name of Pastor Jay Stewart.

FROM JAY

In November of 2015, during one of our meetings to discuss the details of when Derrick would be entrusted with the title and responsibilities of Pastor of The House of Refuge, I felt very stirred and prompted by the Holy Spirit to ask Bishop and Pastor Allen and Derrick and his wife Shonda a weighty question. I had a bona fide WWE wrestling match in my mind and spirit for a good ten minutes, wanting to be sure this prompting was from the Lord. I wanted to be so careful with the relationship of trust and love that had developed between us, never wanting to seem like I had a personal agenda in any of it.

The prompting grew even stronger, until finally I posed the question to them. "Have you all ever had conversations or thoughts about becoming a campus of The Refuge?" There was a brief, awkward pause, then they all looked at each other and started laughing. They said, "Pastor, we talk about it all the time!" We decided then and there to prayerfully explore this together, but it was evident to everyone in my office that the Holy Spirit was present.

Over the next few months we discussed the details of what this could look like and continued to pray together. We began submitting it to the leadership of both churches, and although there were many questions that arose, excitement seemed to rise as well. We had decided that Derrick and Shonda's installation would take place in June of 2016, and I had the high honor of preaching that service in Greensboro. I felt it best to allow Derrick to have a few months to establish his leadership as the new senior pastor, and so we mutually agreed that we would announce the merger in September, and that the merger would become official on November 6, 2016.

The anticipation continued to build as we all sensed the hand of God in this, and it seemed that September 22 couldn't arrive soon enough. The Refuge would be announcing this exciting merger at every location, and in every service at Greensboro, Salisbury, and at the main campus in Concord/Kannapolis, people stood to their feet, releasing shouts of joy and applause. It was so clear to everyone that only the Lord could've orchestrated such a beautiful picture of unity. And only the Lord could've known what would take place less than forty-eight hours later.

On Tuesday afternoon, September 24, a black man was fatally shot by a black Charlotte police officer. Tensions escalated amidst raw emotions, and by the next day people were gathering in the Uptown area of Charlotte to protest. The protestors were incited by outside groups that converged on Charlotte, and within hours things heated to a boiling point. Police in riot gear stood side-by-side in formation as violence erupted, looting ensued, fights broke out, and the city of Charlotte began to resemble a foreign country.

I sat glued to the national news coverage until late in the night with my wife, Melanie, and my two teenaged sons, just twenty miles or so from Uptown. We were in total disbelief. "This cannot be happening in Charlotte," I thought. Still charged with excitement from the announcement we had just made on Sunday, I prayed, "God, there is a better story here that You are writing. Please, somehow get the story of unity out to the masses."

By Thursday things were still in disarray and even more people were crowding into the streets of Uptown, Charlotte. The police and authorities were braced for the worst rioting yet to take place Thursday night. The Refuge had some visiting pastors in town from all over the nation for a pastors' roundtable. Several guys from Texas wanted to grab lunch, and I told them I had just the place—a barbeque joint I thought they would love. Derrick was at the church, and I invited him to join us. I had not been to this particular restaurant in a couple of months, so when I walked in and saw my good friends David and Jason Benham, I instantly knew it was not a coincidence. I greeted them, and they told me they had just flown in that morning from an event. We began talking about the events in Charlotte, and I referenced the announcement I had just made on Sunday. They got very excited and immediately said, "This story needs to get out!" I told them Derrick was with me, and they decided we needed to make a video right then and there. We shot a short video telling the story of unity between two churches, they uploaded it to their Facebook page, and within hours the video went viral. National news outlets picked up the story and began reporting on this "better narrative."

Unity is a priority to God, and it was clear that He wanted our story told. Set to the backdrop of violence, misunderstandings, protests, and hatred, a story of love and trust began to take center stage. Just at the moment Satan thought he had put an exclamation point on the ever-growing racial tensions in America, our great God erased it and put a comma in its place, writing a story that is aligned with His heart—a story that has the potential to bring healing to wounds, beauty from ashes, love where there is hate, and peace where there is strife.

CHAPTER 3

3

THE PRIORITY OF JESUS

FROM JAY

Possibly one of the most sobering experiences in life is to be at the bedside of a person who is near death, preparing at any moment to slip into eternity. Family members and friends will gather around, with much attention given to the final words their loved one will speak. These words carry much weight and linger in the ears and hearts of the recipients like the fragrance of a well-scented candle lingers in the air.

In His final hours, just before Jesus would be stripped, humiliated, spat upon, falsely accused, beaten, and marched through the streets of Jerusalem carrying a rough-hewn cross piece of timber across His lacerated shoulders that would be joined to a larger piece and form a Roman torture device, Jesus prayed. He had been sharing a meal in a room in Jerusalem with His disciples, and then after the meal was complete, Jesus washed their feet and predicted the betrayal of Judas as well as the denial of Peter (John 13). He talked with the disciples about how He is the only avenue to access the Father in relationship, and then promised to send "another comforter," the Holy Spirit (John 14). He admonished them about the importance of love, especially in the context of how the world would treat them (John 15).

I can imagine Jesus then taking a long pause, long enough to cause the disciples to began to shift their sitting or reclining positions on the floor, clear their throats, and look around at each other, wondering what He would say next. I can almost hear the volume of His voice drop as His words took on an even more somber tone. He then proceeded to tell them that He would not be with them much longer, but that it is better that He leave so the Holy Spirit would come (John 16). And then Jesus began praying. He prayed one of the longest and greatest prayers recorded in Scripture. In fact, all of John 17 is His prayer. And in this last prayer before going to the cross, Jesus revealed His priority. We read His words in John 17:20-23:

> I am praying not only for these disciples but also for all who will ever believe in me through their message. I pray that they will all be one, just as you and I are one—as you are in me, Father, and I am in you. And may they be in us so that the world will believe you sent me. I have given them the glory you gave me, so they may be one as we are one. I am in them and you are in me. May they experience such perfect unity that the world will know that you sent me and that you love them as much as you love me.

The word *unity* comes from the Greek word *henótēs*, and it means *oneness* (unity), especially *God-produced unity.*[2] We find this word used in Ephesians 4:3, where Paul writes: "Make every effort to keep the unity of the Spirit through the bond of peace" (NIV). We also find it again in Ephesians 4:13: "until we all reach unity in the faith and in the knowledge of the Son of God and become mature, attaining to the whole measure of the fullness

---

2   Copyright © 1987, 2011 by Helps Ministries, Inc., https://biblehub.com/greek/1775.htm.

of Christ" (NIV).

Notice that nowhere in the Word of God are we told to *create* unity. Why? Very simply, we do not have the ability to do so. Only the Holy Spirit can create unity. We are called to protect and keep what is created by the Holy Spirit. However, we are involved in the process of the Holy Spirit creating unity. I'll explain it with a simple lesson on welding. *The Oxford English Dictionary* defines the word *weld* like this:

Weld:

join together (metal pieces or parts) by heating the surfaces to the point of melting using a blowtorch, electric arc, or other means, and uniting them. Cause to combine and form a harmonious or effective whole.[3]

To weld two pieces of metal together in a way that they will withstand pressure, you start by cleaning the surfaces of each. Rust, dirt, grease, paint, and different coating materials can compromise the integrity of a weld. Paint and certain coating materials will be vaporized when superheated, and this vapor can introduce air bubbles into the weld. All of this can severely compromise the overall strength of the weld.

Second, you have to create the right atmosphere for a proper weld to occur. You do this by introducing gas with a tank of argon and $CO2$. This gas mix shields the weld puddle, displacing impure air and creating an atmosphere for the weld to take place. You can weld without it, but it will gather impurities from the air surrounding it, and typically you'll get poor metal-to-metal burn.

---

3   Oxford English Dictionary, s.v., "weld," accessed September 6, 2020, https://www.lexico.com/en/defini tion/weld.

Third, you need heat or fire. I'll say again, only the Holy Spirit can create unity. We do not have that ability, but when we invite the fire of the Holy Spirit into a pure heart that is protected by the atmosphere of His presence, unity happens!

The Rev. Martin Luther King Jr. once stated the most segregated hour in this nation was at 11:00 a.m. on Sunday morning. For years our country has been divided by something as simple as skin pigmentation. Our nation has tolerated practices like redlining, Jim Crow laws, profiling, unfair voter registration policies, and slavery, further widening the gap between races. We are faced with the task of bringing unity within the Church and our greatly fractured nation. The responsibility to do so does not lie solely on the shoulders of others, but I believe primarily on the shoulders of the Church and those who are Christ-followers. In other words, it is more the job of the church house than it is the White House.

In Proverbs 4:7 (NKJV), we find these instructions from Solomon:

> "Wisdom is the principal thing; therefore get wisdom. And in all your getting, get understanding."

Now notice that Solomon, the wisest man who ever lived, challenges us to go after two things—wisdom and understanding. The pursuit of wisdom will lead us to an understanding, but not to comprehension. I can never comprehend some of the things Derrick has experienced because of racism, but through the help of the Holy Spirit, I can understand how he feels.

In addition to understanding a person from a different background and ethnicity, which comes as a result of listening more than spouting our opinions or ideas, we have to begin building some bridges over the wide expanse of misunderstanding, offense, hatred, prejudice, and division. Building a bridge is important because then there is a connection, an ability to go from one place to another. But the goal moves beyond building a bridge. As long as there is a bridge, you can safely remain where you are and go back and forth as much or as little as you want. There is still separation. I believe God doesn't want us to just bridge the gap, but also to be willing to take the next step.

We have to find ways to permanently close the gap. Peter had a revelation from God that he was to take the gospel to people he had previously thought of as unclean. But he still had to learn to deal with conflict in Acts 15. Fear will often keep us from going any further than just bridging the gap when it comes to racial division. We are afraid of what we will have to give up, or of what God may require from us.

I heard the story of a first grader who went for her first day to a newly integrated school at the height of the segregation storm. An anxious mother met her at the door when she returned home and asked, "How did everything go, honey?"

"Oh Mother! You know what happened? A little black girl sat right next to me!"

In fear and trepidation, the mother expected some trauma, but asked calmly, "And what happened?"

"We were both so scared that we held hands all day."

Suzy Kassem says, "Unity is a beast in itself. If a wolf sees two little boys playing in the woods on one side, and a big strong man on the other, he will go to the one who stands alone."[4] The simple fact is that we are better together. We were made for relationship, and the priority of Jesus is that we close the gap of racism in our nation. The Holy Spirit is the welder, but we have a part in the process. Remember, to weld two pieces of metal together, you start by cleaning each piece. Our job is to repent and allow the blood of Jesus to cleanse us for any part we have played in allowing division, which

---

4 Suzy Kassem, *Rise up and Salute the Sun: The Writings of Suzy Kassem* (Awakened Press, 2011).

breaks His heart, to remain. And I believe repentance is needed on the part of both whites, who have tolerated or contributed to racial disunity, and on the part of blacks, who have refused to forgive or have harbored bitterness and anger for years.

Second, we must create an atmosphere that will allow the Holy Spirit to work. Just like the gas mix creates a shield around the weld puddle and displaces impure air, we need to create an atmosphere conducive to harmony, understanding, and forgiveness, which then drives out the impurities of hatred and division.

Last, and I love this part, we invite the fire of the Holy Spirit into our midst, into relationships, into our fears, and into years of misunderstanding. The fire of His presence forges a bond that cannot be separated. Unity is always a prerequisite to the move of the Holy Spirit. The Holy Spirit was poured out on New Testament believers in Acts 2 because they laid aside their differences, came together in prayer for the sake of the Kingdom, and received the baptism of the Holy Spirit and fire, welding them together under the banner of Jesus, where there is no black, white, yellow, or brown, but everything is red because of His shed blood!

CHAPTER 4

4

UNSUNG HEROES

FROM JAY

Certain things in life have a ripple effect. Much like throwing a rock into a pond, the impact can be seen through the ripples radiating from the point of impact outwardly towards the banks. One person's actions or words can change the course of the lives of others because of what I call the Principle of Outward Impact. It's like the time when I was a teenager and my friend Mark decided to shoot a bottle rocket out of the window of my other friend Rich's car at a pedestrian. But when the sparks burned his hand, he dropped the bottle rocket, which landed on the floorboard of the car and began whizzing around the inside of the car until it exploded with a loud bang. His decision affected all three of us, and there may have been a permanent stain left on the driver's seat.

Obedience has a ripple effect, but so does disobedience. Courage has a ripple effect, and so does fear. Passion has a ripple effect, and so does apathy. Generosity has a ripple effect, and so does selfishness. We see many examples of the Principle of Outward Impact in Scripture through the words and actions of men like David, who defeated a nine-foot-nine-inch giant named Goliath who repeatedly mocked the Israelites to the point that they were paralyzed and shaking in their sandals. David's underdog defeat of this ruthless, overgrown Philistine secured victory for the entire nation of Israel, not just for himself.

Similarly, one cannot help but think of the courageous exploits of Queen Esther. This young girl won a yearlong beauty contest and was chosen to replace Vashti as Queen of Persia. Through her uncle Mordecai, she became privy to a wicked plot to destroy all Jews throughout the 127 provinces that stretched from India to Ethiopia. Mordecai admonished Esther to approach King Xerxes and plead for her people. There were risks involved. Anyone appearing in his inner court without being invited was doomed to die unless he extended his gold scepter to them. Mordecai then reminded Esther of the Principle of Outward Impact in Esther 4:13-14:

> "Don't think for a moment that because you're in the palace you will escape when all other Jews are killed. If you keep quiet at a time like this, deliverance and relief for the Jews will arise from some other place, but you and your relatives will die. Who knows if perhaps you were made queen for just such a time as this?"

If you are familiar with the story, the King did extend his scepter to Esther, she informed him of the vile and evil plot of Haman, and the Jewish people were spared throughout the land—the ripple effect of courage.

If we step outside of the stories of the Bible for a moment, we find real-life examples of the courageous words and actions of people who sent ripples throughout the civil rights movement in America. Our nation sets aside a national holiday in January each year to commemorate the life and work of Dr. Martin Luther King Jr. We celebrate the decision Rosa Parks made the evening of December 1, 1955, when she refused, after a long day of work as a seamstress in Montgomery, Alabama, to give up her seat on a public bus.

We discuss in detail in chapter 8 the selfless act of the Greensboro Four—Joseph McNeil, Franklin McCain, Ezell Blair Jr., and David Richmond. Their decision affected not just their lives, but the lives of hundreds of thousands because of the Principle of Outward Impact.

Our society draws attention to and celebrates the acts of celebrities, athletes, entrepreneurs, politicians, and philanthropists, and often with good reason. But I am equally inspired by the people who have done things, both in Scripture and in the civil rights movement, that very few people have heard about—the unsung heroes. The exploits of some of these unsung heroes from Scripture are inspiring to say the least. They affected many lives, yet the sad reality is that most people have never heard of them. Allow me to highlight a few:

BENAIAH – His highlight reel would be pretty short if it were running on the local news. We do not find many mentions of him in the Bible. But his bravery prepared him for a key role in the many battles that King David would lead the armies of Israel to fight. In one of Benaiah's prelims, he took on two Moabite champion fighters. Another time, he found himself in the octagon with an Egyptian warrior. Benaiah had a club, and the Egyptian had a spear. Not much of a fair fight, but Benaiah somehow managed to wrestle the spear away from the Egyptian and then proceeded to kill him with it. Oh, and then there was the time Benaiah chased a lion into some sort of pit while it was snowing. Are you kidding me? While on a safari in Tanzania once, we came upon a lion that had just taken down a cape buffalo. There was not one millisecond that I contemplated jumping out of the Land Rover and running towards him. But these acts of courage prepared Benaiah for his greater assignment, which was to become the head of David's secret service.

SHIPHRAH AND PUAH – The Israelites were in slavery to the Egyptians for 400 years, and over the course of time the Israelites, according to Exodus 1:7, "multiplied so greatly that they became extremely powerful and filled the land." A new king came into power and decided it was time to reduce the Israelite population. He gave instructions to the Israelite midwives, including Shiphrah and Puah, to kill the male babies as they were born. However, the Bible says that these two unsung heroes feared God more than they feared this pharaoh (Exodus 1:17), so they let the babies live, thus helping to preserve the nation of Israel.

JEHOIADA – We cannot leave this guy out. Joash is known as one of the greatest kings of Judah. He reigned for forty years and did many notable things to restore true worship, abolish idolatry, and rebuild the Temple. But if not for Jehoiada, it never would have happened. A very wicked woman named Athaliah, the daughter of King Ahab and Queen Jezebel, appointed herself ruler of Judah, and at the top of her to-do list was killing off any descendant of David. But God had promised David that one of his descendants would always be on the throne. And it is even bigger than the throne of Jerusalem—God promised to send the world a Savior from the line of David. A heroic aunt and uncle scooped up an infant named Joash while Athaliah was on her killing rampage and hid him in the Temple for six years. If Joash died, then the promise of a Savior from David's lineage would also die. In 2 Chronicles 23:11 we read, "Then Jehoiada and his sons brought out Joash, the king's son, placed the crown on his head, and presented him with a copy of God's laws. They anointed him and proclaimed him king, and everyone shouted, 'Long live the king!'"

Imagine how different the path of history would look if not for the acts of these and many other unsung heroes in Scripture. Their decisions had a ripple effect for centuries and still affect our lives today. In the same way, were it not for the courageous acts of many unsung heroes of the civil rights movement, history would look much different, as would our nation today.

FROM DERRICK

When I think about the people who have impacted my life and our nation, it is not the most popular people or those who have done the most. It is usually the ones who have been effective in small ways that leave a lasting impression.

When I was twenty-three years old, I was given what I believe was one of the strangest prophetic words. It was from a lady affectionately known as Mother Allen, a loving mother, grandmother, and a woman of prayer. She was one of the sweetest and most compassionate people you would ever meet. She had a quality about her that drew people who came to glean from her words, words that were weighted and dripping with wisdom. She stayed in a little brick house that her husband built. It did not possess great curb appeal, nor did she have the best furniture. She wasn't a preacher, and she did not have a background in theology. Yet people would come just to latch on to her wisdom.

One day while sitting at her house, she gave me what I felt was an unattractive word from the Lord. She looked at me as she sat in her slightly worn chair, with her piercing eyes that could see into your soul. Her skin was withered and her voice as soft as a feather as she whispered, "Darling, you are going to be effective!"

What type of word is that? I thought to myself. Why couldn't it have been that I was going to be rich and powerful, or something other than "effective"? I was very unimpressed, to say the least, and somewhat immature in my understanding of God. I never looked up the definition of the word *effective*, and honestly felt disconnected from the word completely. In my immaturity and frustration I basically discarded her words, telling myself she really missed God's voice.

It was not until I was in my thirties that the definition of the word *effective* would be significant in my life, causing me to remember and appreciate her words. Webster's defines *effective* as: "successful in producing a decided, decisive, or desired effect."[5] Unsung heroes are individuals who often fly under the radar, people who may not have the best education or even become the face of a movement, but are successful in producing results. The Bible is filled with people whom many might consider to be the least likely to succeed. Some of us may feel like Saul, who did not stand out in a crowd, or like David, who was hidden in a field. If we are not careful, we will overlook and miss some of the most impactful people due to our deeply skewed perspective.

In the mid-1950s, the civil rights movement began, which changed the course of this country. During this time racial prejudice and hatred covered our nation, resulting in many people being hung, beaten, and falsely accused. These individuals never had the chance to make it to prominence, but their blood and sacrifices were not wasted. On February 1, 1960, a sit-in movement began in Greensboro, North Carolina, at the counter of the Woolworth's Department Store located at 132 South Elm Street. It was initiated by four young black men who were students at North Carolina Agricultural and Technical University. As impressed as I am with the actions of the Greensboro Four, I am equally impressed with the courage of many high school students who rose to support the sit-in. Students from Dudley High School, located a few miles from North Carolina A&T, played a significant role in the sit-in movement when the college students returned home for the summer. These young students chose to sit in their stead, fiercely protecting what the four young college men had initiated. Some were thrown in jail, while others were threatened. Though these lo-

5   Merriam-Webster, s.v. "effective," accessed September 6, 2020, https://www.merriam-webster.com/dictionary/effective.

cal students' names might not have made the history books, these unsung heroes were just as vital as the four young men who began the peaceful protests.

People like Rosa Parks and Dr. King Jr are often considered to be the faces of the civil rights movement, and truly they were some of the most courageous people to ever live. Yet as much as history was shaped by them, the civil rights movement would not have begun without people like Mammie Till-Mobley. She was the mother of Emmett Till, a fourteen-year-old young man from Chicago who was murdered for simply whistling at a married white woman in Money, Mississippi. His mother made the choice to have an open casket funeral to show how two white men brutally beat her son, mutilated his body, and threw him in the Tallahatchie River. Mississippi officials tried their best to prevent the body from being shown, but Mammie Till-Mobley fought to ensure his body was brought back to Chicago where they lived. She stated: "I want the world to see what they did to my boy."[6] More than 100,000 people viewed the body of Emmett Till. At the time, it was the largest civil rights demonstration in American history. Mammie wasn't trying to change history; she was a grieving mother who wanted to see justice for her son. Some, however, would say that her courage and resolve changed the course of history. Mammie Till fought against the injustice of underserved and underprivileged black children until her death in 2003. She kept fighting even though she never found justice for her own child.[7]

Then there was the Tougaloo Nine. Undoubtedly inspired by the courage of the Greensboro Four, these nine students, five African American males and four African American females, who were part of the Tougaloo NAACP youth council, participated in Mississippi's first civil rights "read-in" at the whites-only Jackson Municipal Public Library.

6   "Historian recalls moment Emmett Till's accuser admitted she lied," CBS News, January 31, 2017, https://www.cbsnews.com/news/the-blood-of-emmett-till-carolyn-bryant-lied-timothy-tyson-new-book/.

7   Mamie-Till Mobley, *Mississippi Encyclopedia*, https://mississippiencyclopedia.org/entries/marnie-till-mobley/.

On March 27, 1961, these nine students walked into a segregated municipal library in Jackson, Mississippi, to complete an assignment for a class project. After they refused to move from the segregated library, the library attendant called the police. The students were thrown out of the library, arrested, and given a $100 dollar fine and a 30-day suspended sentence. This sit-in drew support from African American colleges like Tougaloo College, but also from predominantly white colleges like Millsaps College in Mississippi.[8]

Unsung heroes are not looking for their names to be plastered for all to see with a desire to make history, but they do want to change history. I still think about the words Mother Allen spoke over me when she said, "You will be effective." Effective people desire to see results even if it means they never receive credit. For some African Americans, our ancestors were not allowed to learn to read as slaves. Some had little to no education. The Tougaloo Nine helped make it possible for African Americans to have access to libraries and to be able to read with people of other ethnicities. It is important to remember that the very things we often take for granted, someone fought for. We still have an opportunity to write history today.

FROM JAY

What do heroes really look like? Take a look in the mirror, and you will see. Heroes are most often just common, ordinary people. But they do possess a few distinguishing characteristics.

1. **UNSUNG HEROES ARE NOT BORN BUT DEVELOPED**. A man was visiting various cities in Europe, many of which were known as the birthplace of great artists, musicians, composers, and kings. In one particular city, while sitting on a park bench, he asked a local resident,

---

8   The Tougaloo Nine, *Black Past*, October 6, 2019, https://www.blackpast.org/african-american-history/the-tougaloo-nine-1961/.

"Were any great celebrities or famous people born here?" The resident replied, "Nope, just babies." In his book *If Only*, Dr. Neal Roese makes a distinction between two types of regret: regrets of action and regrets of inaction.[9] Unsung heroes are proactive, always looking for opportunities to develop into the image of God. They run towards challenges and not away from them, knowing that God will use difficulties to prepare them for something greater.

2. **UNSUNG HEROES ARE NOT FLAWLESS OR FEARLESS, BUT THEY ARE COURAGEOUS.** Half of learning is learning, and half of learning is un-learning. But un-learning is twice as hard. Our minds have infected files that must be defragged like a computer with a virus. It is harder to get old thoughts out than it is to get new thoughts in. There are approximately 2,000 classified fears. For example, there is zemmiphobia, which is the fear of the great mole rat. There is papaphobia, or fear of the Pope. Then there is helminthophobia, or the fear of being infested with worms. There is also linonophobia, which is the fear of string. What is so interesting is that psychiatrists say we are born with only two innate fears: fear of falling and fear of loud noises. All other fears are learned, which means they can be unlearned.

The alternative to fear for many is boredom. Many Christ-followers have settled for a life of boredom rather than moving ahead in courage in spite of fear that tries to immobilize and paralyze. Soren Kierkegaard says that ". . . boredom is the root of all evil."[10]

3. **UNSUNG HEROES ARE NOT ABOUT PROMOTION, BUT PRODUCTION.** Our ultimate destiny is determined by whether or not we seize the God-ordained opportunities presented to us. If we do, it starts a

---

9   Neal Roese, *If Only: How to Turn Regret into Opportunity* (Harmony, 2005).

10 https://www.goodreads.com/quotes/8343184-boredom-is-the-root-of-all-evil-it-is-very.

chain reaction. If we fail to seize them, we short-circuit God's plan and momentum in our lives. Unsung heroes are not focused on what will benefit them the most, or on avoiding problems. They want what is best for the Kingdom and for humanity. Success is like your fingerprint, unique to who you are and different from others. But the pattern for success for all of us is always traced back to mustard-seed opportunities of faithfulness. Success is doing the best you can with what you have where you are.

FROM DERRICK

I am often asked by individuals who desire to help narrow the racial divide, "What can we do?" I am in no way an expert, but there are some things I feel are helpful for those who genuinely want to move the lines. We can begin by educating ourselves on the brutal history of our nation, changing the narrative and choosing compassion. Some things are hard to hear and at times even harder to stomach. Keep in mind, if it's hard for you to hear, just imagine how hard it was for Mammie Till to see her son's body beaten and mutilated. The truth is hard, and we must be committed to hearing the truth and accepting all that comes with it. We also have a responsibility to do our part. I challenge you to be willing to have tough conversations and to attempt to get to know the stories of our history.

CHANGING THE NARRATIVE

As for Pastor Jay and I, in the midst of adversity and the political divide in our country, we are choosing to write a better narrative, and that comes with challenges. We seek to educate our staff by showing them the history of our country as we take ownership of our part in it. We teach about diversity and equality. We choose to live a multiethnic life beyond having a diverse church, embracing the very things that make us different as well as the things that make us the same. We learn about each other's culture and find ways to embrace it. Pastor Jay recently took our entire pastoral team to the International Civil Rights Center and Museum, located in the old Woolworth's building on 132 South Elm Street in Greensboro. Learning about and embracing some of the Negro hymns such as "Wade in the Water" and "Roll Jordan Roll," which served as codes and directives for slaves to guide them to meeting spots as they attempted to flee bondage to freedom, is important. Other things, like the Negro National Anthem and our preaching styles are important to the African American culture.

We cannot live in a diverse world and continue to live segregated lives, allowing our race to continue to divide us. As an African American father who is raising sons, I choose to change the narrative by the way I live out my life before them. I admonish you to do life with people who do not look like you, who may not share the same economic background or even education as you. Let's build relationships beyond the things that divide us, realizing, probably more than we actually know, that we are all the same kind of different.

MAKE THE CHOICE

We have to choose to look through someone else's echo chamber, feeling compassion when we see African American children slain in our streets or see people profiled and pulled over because of the color of their skin. We can choose to fight against mass incarceration and redlining and to not ignore injustices we see. Begin by asking the Holy Spirit to reveal anything in your heart that may have bias toward another race or even prejudice that may be underlying your attitudes. I believe that one individual deciding to seek a better today can change the lives of millions of others tomorrow. Today I choose to be an unsung hero, not seeking to make history but to make a difference in the world by doing my part. What choices will you make? Unity is a battle that requires a resolute decision to stay in the fight no matter how hard things get.

Mother Allen was one of my unsung heroes, along with Anna Jones and Ella Odessa Bost. I can still hear the sweet whisper of Mother Allen's voice, and the alto vibration in the voice of Anna, my great-grandmother, as she would sing songs of freedom. I am thankful for the memory of seeing my grandmother Ella on her knees, crying out to God to save us. These are not names that you would be even remotely familiar with, but they helped to lay the foundation for my life. They never had a chance to be featured on national television or written about in articles or periodicals. Yet it was their words and resilience in the face of adversity, their singing of hymns and powerful spirit-filled prayers, that shaped me and made me proud of my heritage. Some of them served white families and barely made enough to take care of their own children, but their faith and courage provides a platform that allows us to stand on their shoulders. They were some of the ones who could not use certain restrooms or eat in certain restaurants. And now I feel I owe it to them to continue to fight and keep moving forward so that their sacrifice, courage, and work is not in vain.

This work doesn't come without tears, sacrifice, and labor pains. There will be times you will ask yourself if it's even worth it. But unsung heroes must be willing to take the risk even if it means not seeing the reward in your lifetime. Often when someone is being used to change history they don't realize it. In fact, it may feel that little to no progress is being made. However, the struggle has a way of purifying our motives and keeping our agenda focused on the only One who can truly empower us to bring about lasting change—Jesus!

CHAPTER 5

CHAPTER

5

WE ARE BETTER TOGETHER

FROM JAY

We have all had moments in life when we see something and immediately think, *There is a story behind that!* Like the time I saw a woman in the airport preparing to catch her flight, dressed in a cat costume with a long cat tail attached to her rear end that was sliding across the floor behind her. Or the time I passed a woman in an upscale mall carrying a monkey on her shoulder. These are the things in life that make you go, "Hmm . . ."

I had relatives who lived in the small, rural southeast Alabama town of Brundidge. Sometime around the summer of 1974 we paid a visit to Brundidge, and on the way back to Columbus we stopped in Enterprise, Alabama. My uncle was a helicopter pilot in the United States Army and was stationed at the time in Fort Rucker, just outside of Enterprise. Now there wasn't much to do in Enterprise, and there certainly wasn't much to hold the attention of an eleven-year-old boy. However, I do remember stopping in downtown Enterprise to see a statue. Fashioned by an Italian sculptor and dedicated in December of 1919, this white marble statue of a beautiful woman stands over thirteen feet tall, and certainly makes one think, *There is a story behind that!*

You may be thinking, *What's so odd about a marble statue of a beautiful woman in the middle of a small town?* It's a fair question. The oddity is what she is holding above her head: she is hoisting a large bowl, and inside the bowl is an insect called a boll weevil that single-handedly wiped out the cotton crop of much of the south in the early 1900s. Possibly odder than the statue is what is written on the plaque that stands at its base. It reads, "In profound appreciation of the boll weevil and what it has done as the herald of prosperity this monument was erected by the citizens of Enterprise, Coffee County, Alabama." Theodore Roosevelt touted the weevil as a "blessing in disguise." Why?

To understand these statements about the insect that destroyed the primary industry of this southeast Alabama town, we have to go back several years. The weevils, no bigger than a pinky fingernail, were a cotton farmer's worst nightmare—a nightmare that came true for thousands across the South starting in 1892. That was the year the insect, a native of Mexico, first crossed the Rio Grande near Brownsville, Texas.

But the story of how God was at work goes back even further, to the year 1864 in a place called Diamond, Missouri, where a boy was born into slavery. He was given the name George, and his owner's wife, Susan, broke protocol when she decided to teach young George to read and write. Being somewhat sick and frail, George wasn't able to contribute much in terms of working on the farm, but Susan taught him to cook and garden. At a young age, George took a very keen interest in plants, experimenting with natural pesticides and soil conditioners. As he continued to grow, it was evident that George had a curiosity and a propensity for learning. It is interesting to consider the tapestry of destiny that God was weaving throughout the events of his life, bringing different people along at key times to help prepare him to fulfill a most unexpected assignment. At age eleven, George left the farm to attend an all-black school in a nearby town. He was taken in by Andrew and Mariah Watkins, an African American couple with no children of their own. Mariah taught George two things that would stay with him the rest of his life: her knowledge of medicinal herbs and her faith in God. He went on to graduate in 1880 from Minneapolis High School in Minneapolis, Kansas, and then applied for enrollment to Highland College in Kansas. He was initially accepted, but when the school administration learned he was black they rejected his admission.

George then enrolled in Simpson College and studied art and piano. But when a professor by the name of Etta Budd discovered his love of botany, she encouraged him to apply for admission to Iowa State University. In 1894, George made history by becoming the first African American to graduate from Iowa State. He continued his graduate studies and earned his Master of Agriculture degree in 1896. Now the story gets even more interesting.

Offers began pouring in, including one from Booker T. Washington, the founder and president of Tuskegee Institute (now Tuskegee University) in Tuskegee, Alabama. George Carver accepted the offer to be the head of the agricultural department and would later even add the name Washington to his own name. George felt destiny unfolding and recognized that God had gifted him in the area of botany for a greater purpose. He immediately began studying crop rotations as the scourge of the boll weevil continued to make its way across the southern states, leaving a path of destruction in its wake. By 1909, the weevil had reached nearby Mobile County, Alabama. Cotton was their main cash crop, and with the weevils now in their fields, farmers were getting smaller and smaller yields. In addition, cotton depleted the soil of much-needed nutrients, making it difficult for other crops to grow in its place.

Carver knew that peanuts were one of the few plants that could thrive in the depleted soil, and more and more farmers bought into the idea of replacing their cotton with peanuts. By the year 1917, farmers near

Enterprise produced over one million bushels of peanuts that sold for more than five million dollars, and by 1919, Coffee County was the largest producer of peanuts in the nation. Carver discovered over three hundred uses for the peanut, including flour, paste, insulation, paper, wall board, wood stains, soap, shaving cream, medicines, and skin lotion. Today, Carver is credited with saving the agricultural economy of the rural South.

I find it interesting that God raised up an African American man, born into slavery, who would be trained and prepared to relocate to the Deep South to help predominantly white rural farmers. I find it interesting that God would make "beauty out of ashes" from the destruction of a small insect by leading farmers to greater prosperity, and by leading George Carver to eighty-eight patents in one year. In all likelihood, neither would have happened were it not for the boll weevil. Is it possible that God was trying to show mankind in the early 1900s that we are really better together? And is it possible that in the midst of the division and destruction in our nation brought on by racism, God again wants us to realize that we are better together?

You may have heard the story of the contest that took place at a county fair to see which horse could pull the most weight. A large muscular thoroughbred was hitched to the weighted sled and managed to pull over 800 pounds the measured-out length of 150 feet. His most fierce competition would prove to be a young paint horse. This massive animal proceeded to pull 1,000 pounds across the line. A few onlookers began to ponder what would happen if they were working together. The two horses were yoked together. The natural assumption would be that they would pull 1,800 pounds together. However, to everyone's shock, these two horses working together were able to pull 2,200 pounds of weight the full distance.

Regardless of our skin color, we were made for relationship, and we can only thrive in the context of relationship with others. We will never fully discover our purpose and destiny in isolation. If unity is indeed the prerequisite for revival, as we discussed in chapter three, how much have we limited the plans of God for our nation by refusing to work with someone who has a different ethnicity or skin color? And how much has this grieved the heart of God?

I love the powerful words we read in Psalm 133:

> *How good and pleasant it is*
> *when God's people live together in unity!*
> *It is like precious oil poured on the head,*
> *running down on the beard,*
> *running down on Aaron's beard,*
> *down on the collar of his robe.*
> *It is as if the dew of Hermon*
> *were falling on Mount Zion.*
> *For there the LORD bestows his blessing,*
> *even life forevermore.*

This unity that produces the blessing of God is precious and worth protecting, but it requires work on our part. According to Scripture there is a key, something we must be willing to do in order to experience the commanded blessing of God.

We must learn to celebrate and not just tolerate differences.

Diversity was God's idea. The church in Colossae was dealing with some bona fide challenges brought on by diversity, and Paul addresses these in chapter three of the book of Colossians. They had an attitude of tolerating and not celebrating. Greeks and Jews, circumcised and uncircumcised, foreigners and Scythians (who were known as very wild and cruel people) had all come into relationship with Christ, but they had brought different religious practices with them. The Jerusalem Council that took place around AD 50 was called to address these differences, but the church was still dealing with them in Colossae. Paul wanted them to understand that protecting unity doesn't mean we all conform to one thing. But it does mean that we all commit to one Man, Jesus. If we do that, our differences will mean very little and we will learn to celebrate them together as we focus on Jesus.

In Psalm 133, the first two verses describe an anointing oil that flows over the head, beard, and robe of the priest. The word for anointing is *shemen*, which means "to make fat, to satisfy, and to increase." Living together in unity with others brings an increase of the anointing of the Holy Spirit into your life, and it attracts the blessing of God. An African proverb says, "When there is no enemy within, the enemies outside cannot hurt you." One of the most Christlike, anointed, godly, and powerful things you can do is to live in harmony with others in the body of Christ, celebrate the differences, and walk arm in arm to advance the Kingdom of God. God is not looking for uniformity, but He does expect unity. And when we learn to appreciate and celebrate our differences, we discover the powerful principle that we are better together.

CHAPTER

6

CHAPTER

6

PIECES/PĒS

FROM DERRICK

When you hear the word *piece*, what comes to mind? When someone asks for a "piece" of anything, something has to happen in order for you to fulfill that request. Usually you have to tear one thing apart, dividing it into two separate entities in order to give one part away and keep the other part for yourself. If someone has a "piece of your heart," what that means in the grand scheme of things is that they don't have all of your heart. The giver offers a specifically calculated percentage, purposefully reserving enough to have the ability to give another percentage to someone else should the need or request arise. When your wife asks you for a piece of your pizza, or a bite of your dessert, what does that mean? It means she's going to eat ALL of it. Understand and make no mistake about it: this is the only example where *piece* means ALL instead of some.

As I researched the word "piece" and "pieces," I saw a consistent pattern. You cannot get a piece of anything without breaking something, cutting something, tearing something, or dividing something into fragments. Most of our lives have reflected this definition to some degree. We have been torn, broken, ripped, and fragmented. We have often not felt whole. We search for someone or something to put the pieces of our heart or our lives back together again, trying our best to manage life and make sense of a puzzle with missing pieces.

As much as I hate putting puzzles together, I love the reward of seeing the image in its fulness when all the pieces are connected. But one of the reasons I hate the process is because it takes time. It takes a lot of concentration. It requires trial and error. It demands patience. Most people who begin putting puzzles together want to see the end of a thing from the beginning. The picture on the box is appealing because it shows us that wholeness is possible. It provides a glimpse of what can be, coupled with a truth we don't always want to admit: *if we keep working at it, eventually everything will come together.* What do you do when the pieces of your life seem to be harder to put back together? How do you move forward when you feel like your puzzle box has missing pieces? How do you cope with the reality that the puzzle someone else has been given is easier to put together than yours because they have fewer pieces and the "corners" are more obvious than yours?

Comparison is a purpose killer. Comparison distorts your discernment and ruins your uniqueness. When you continue to view your life through the lens of comparison, you will never reach a place of peace with your pieces. It can be discouraging and overwhelming when you first start the process. If you are like me, you may have looked at the pieces of your life and wondered, "What have I gotten myself into?" But eventually, if you stay focused and committed to the process, you will see light at the end of the tunnel. You will also be able to eliminate counterfeit pieces that don't belong in your box. Let's go a little deeper.

noun: piece
plural noun: pieces

a portion of an object or of material, produced by cutting, tearing, or breaking the whole.[11]

I am convinced that every piece of our lives—each disappointment, rejection, pain, shame, joy, sorrow, mistake, accomplishment, year, fear, love, and lesson—is essential to us becoming the whole person that God called us to be. From the beginning of time God had a plan. He has placed people into your life strategically and intentionally. Think for a moment about how the Bible was constructed. In the beginning, God created the heavens and the earth. He formed Adam from the ground knowing that Adam would fail. Sin was no surprise to our sovereign God. Jesus wasn't an "oops" rescue mission project. Jesus was a part of the process from the beginning. But in order for us to appreciate Jesus for who He is, God the Father had to strategically introduce His piece of salvation after forty-two generations of failure, forty-two generations of mistakes, and forty-two generations of man attempting to fix the sin issue, yet always falling short.

Nothing catches God by surprise. He knows your frame. He knows your name. He knew you would do what you did, and He devised a plan that would make it possible for your name to be written in the Lamb's Book of Life. God is not shocked by your mistakes. He has planned grace for every mistake and mercy for every moment. This is the beauty of the big picture. From eternity, God calls us into time. He uses our brokenness as an opportunity to draw us closer to Himself.

---

11 Oxford English Dictionary, s.v. "piece," https://www.lexico.com/definition/piece.

If we understand this truth, then we will not dismiss or discount the moments of brokenness. Instead, we will see that even our brokenness can be a tool God uses to help us become who we were always called to be.

Looking back over our life and surveying the picture we endeavor to create with God's help, we begin to realize that every tear was purposeful. Every cut was useful. Every letdown you experienced was necessary. Why? Because it propelled you into your destiny. This is a truth that I have experienced in my own life. I know this to be fact through personal experience. As I was lying, strapped to a bed in a mental institution, I assumed that my life was over. I sat there thinking a multitude of things, but most of the time, I found myself asking many questions. *God, how can I recover from this? God, how did I get here? God, what am I living for? Will you ever use a man as flawed as me?* In everything I had done up until that point, I had some level of control regarding the outcome. I chose to rob and steal. I chose to drink. I chose not to obey God. And I chose to run from my calling. This was the first time I knew that God controlled the next move. I could not walk away. I couldn't mask my emotions with alcohol or marijuana. This was the closest I had ever been to taking my life. For years I had buried all my feelings. I had suppressed my emotions and told myself, *You'll be all right if you just go to bed and wake up the next morning.* But now I was at the point of explosion.

Have you ever been at the point of explosion? Have you ever looked around and realized that nothing was the same? Everything you once depended on is gone, and now it is just you and God. Have you ever been at a breaking point where not even your kids or your family had enough power or influence to keep you from making a harmful decision? That was where I found myself. The doctors explained to me that I had experienced a psychotic breakdown. But I knew the truth: I was at the end of my rope. I was tired of the pain and exhausted with life. I was done with having to figure things out. I had buried my feelings long enough, and now those suppressed emotions began to rumble inside and eventually erupted like a volcano. I stayed in the hospital for ten long days. While there, every piece of my life flashed before my eyes. I thought about the drugs, the sex, the money, the lies, the betrayal, and the hurt. My mind was constantly flooded with the thoughts of deferred hope, the harm, the fear, the risks, the questions, and the lack of answers. All of it flashed before me. I had to confront the pieces as they came. I was accustomed to avoiding hard things. I had taught myself how to compartmentalize my emotions. This time, however, I could not run from myself. I had to search for the root cause of all my pain.

I began to realize that much of it was rooted in hurt and disappointment that stemmed from my mom. For years I had buried the pain of what I felt toward my biological mother, but now was the time for me to come to grips with these pieces. The truth is, I felt unloved. I felt discarded. With deep pain, I had to admit that she never really wanted us, and as a result of her rejection of me, I felt the pain of abandonment. Her absence from my life was more palpable than the presence of others in my life.

A great blessing is that I didn't have to work this all out on my own. I had three siblings who were dealing with some of the same emotions. My sister was displaced at the age of three, and I never saw her again until I was thirteen. When I finally did see her as a teenager, I barely remembered her. My brother, on the other hand, was raised by his father. Other than our physical resemblance, we have very little in common. My youngest brother was the only son whom my mom kept, but he suffered just as badly being with her. All of us were trying to put the pieces of our lives together without the mother who brought us into this world.

This pain from my childhood bled into every relationship that I had. We should not be surprised when the pain of disappointment and the dysfunctions of our childhood show up in our adulthood. In the world today, there are millions of fathers and mothers who are trying to parent children, yet they never had the example or model of healthy parents themselves.

Many men and women are the way they are because their puzzle called life came with some missing pieces of affection, attention, encouragement, protection, and compassion. I forgive my mother for what she did. I choose to not blame her for how I suffered.

Moving toward health and healing required me to face the hard truth I was struggling to admit—I was starved for love, and I was looking for someone to be the mom I never had. I was bleeding onto innocent bystanders in search of a mother's touch. And because it never happened as a young boy and teen, I learned to manage life with missing pieces. When I met girls, I didn't know how to have a healthy relationship with them. Nor did I know how to treat them like royalty. I could not love them, even though I tried, because I did not truly love myself. I made each one an idol of some sort, expecting them to love me in a way that I had longed for from my mother. I really had little comprehension of how to give or even express love. I was broken, and the icing on the cake happened when my step-grandfather, Charlie, kicked me out of the only safe place I had known with my grandmother. The abandonment turned into bitterness and more disappointment.

As I lay there looking at the padded white walls in the mental institution, I tried to escape by breaking through the straps placed on my wrists. I was a prisoner of my own pain, and there was no one in my life to bail me out. I wasn't just trying to get out of the room—I was trying to stop reliving the past in my head. Every scene that was replayed in my mind brought back another painful memory. I thought about how Charlie told me I had to leave and how I cried all the way to my dad's house. From there the scene jumped to me looking for hours at my stillborn son lying fully dressed. Staring at his tiny fingers and feet, time stood still and I went numb. Seeing all the features he had and how much he favored me, I could not help but feel like a part of me died when he died.

I was reminded of how many mistakes I had made. As each scene flashed in my mind, regret filled my heart. The attendants tried to hold me down and gave me medication to keep me calm, but nothing worked. Nurses resorted to jabbing a long needle into my arm containing a stronger medicine they hoped would sedate me, and eventually I fell asleep. Dreams and nightmares came. At some point I woke up to the memory of me faking my graduation and of the abortion I forced my girlfriend to have. I heard her tears. I heard her crying. I heard her pleading with me not to make her go through with it. I thought about the enormous pain I had inflicted on my family. It seemed to never stop, even for a moment. I was totally at fault, and I could not escape the guilt and the grief. I cried for days, embarrassed one minute and angry the next.

I knew that in order to come out on the side of healing and health, I had to be real and honest, with myself and with others. The truth for anyone is that you cannot change your past. What is done is done. The challenge now is figuring out how you will learn from it and move forward. The pieces of our lives are not just comprised of our mistakes; they are also comprised of moments that have shaped us for a particular purpose. I look back over all of the painful moments, all of the mistakes I made and that others made that affected me, and I realize that my response to it all and my willingness to surrender completely to the Lord has given me the ability to forgive others. And it has produced a larger capacity in me to love others with true compassion. I can be an agent of hope and healing in the area of racial reconciliation because I did not allow the painful and unfair moments and seasons of life to destroy my purpose and destiny.

Every human being, regardless of skin color, is made with great thought, intentionality, and uniqueness by the hands of God. Psalm 139 says that each person is "fearfully and wonderfully made." I began to realize that when God made me, He made me beautiful, in His image. I also began to realize that every event, every mistake, and every piece that would make up the mosaic of my life was sculpted with an intention. These moments would become authentic works of art that God would use to tell my story, all for His glory. And He will do the same for you. He has an ability like no one else to make beauty from ashes.

The culmination of all of the pieces really beginning to come together happened on August 14, 2003. I had been invited by my friend Joe to a service at Dorsett Chapel, a small church in Spencer, North Carolina. As I approached the grounds, I felt something different. This was two days before I was admitted to the Broughton Mental Facility and all of the things I just shared took place. As I entered the church that night, I knew I would not leave the same as I was upon arriving. It seemed as if every word the preacher spoke that night was a piece from the puzzle of my life. The Bible literally opened up to me and came alive. This middle-aged, dark-skinned man gave an altar call at the end of his powerful message. It was as though something pulled me out of my seat and at that moment, I could no longer hear or see anyone else. I felt as if God had marked this moment in time for me to have a powerful encounter with Him.

YOU'VE BEEN MARKED

As the pastor gave an invitation for anyone who wanted to rededicate their life to Christ, tears began to flow down my face. I knew this was my moment, and I knew this was a major piece of my life falling into place. I walked toward the front, and a sea of hugs and hands were extended. I felt the presence of God again as a piece of my heart come back to life. I felt the same feeling I had felt at the age of twelve while attending Henderson Grove Baptist Church. I knew I could no longer run, and I didn't want to, except straight into His arms. My heart was gripped with an unbelievable feeling of awe and emotion. This was the piece I had been missing.

I remembered Grandma Anna rocking in her chair on the front porch of her old house, humming and singing songs about Jesus. I remembered her gray hair and freckled face, and how she would sing and talk about God, and I couldn't help but listen. Now I was experiencing the same feeling I had when I listened to her as she shared her love of God with me. I often wondered as a young boy if I would ever have that same experience. It seemed as if every traumatic experience I had endured was instantly erased during that altar call moment. Without hesitation, I said yes to God once and for all. This was the call I had been running from. But on that hot August night, I embarked on a new journey.

This wasn't the first time I had responded to the altar call and said yes to the Lord. But times prior to this night I had often been motivated by guilt. On this night I was drawn by the Holy Spirit. I found the peace I needed and let go of every insecurity that I had held on to and every memory that held me captive. Our memories are a combination of good and bad experiences, and we all have to make a decision regarding them. We either choose to allow each piece of our story to bring us to a place of surrender, or we choose to remain in continued rebellion. You can use your past as a means to justify your refusal to change, or you can use every part to heal you and lead you to wholeness in God.

In Scripture, there is a Hebrew word used to describe the moment Moses realized he could no longer run away from his assignment. It is the word . . .

Hineni,
which means "Here am I."

The story is found in Exodus 3:1-4.

> One day Moses was tending the flock of his father-in-law, Jethro, the priest of Midian. He led the flock far into the wilderness and came to Sinai, the mountain of God. There the angel of the Lord appeared to him in a blazing fire from the middle of a bush. Moses stared in amazement. Though the bush was engulfed in flames, it didn't burn up. "This is amazing," Moses said to himself. "Why isn't that bush burning up? I must go see it."
>
> When the Lord saw Moses coming to take a closer look, God called to him from the middle of the bush, "Moses! Moses!"
>
> "Here I am!" Moses replied.

Moses had been running for the last forty years of his life in an effort to escape his past, only to discover that even though he was hiding in the desert, he could not escape the omnipresence of God. I was doing the same thing. But God found me, and I came to a place of full surrender to Him. In my state of brokenness, in spite of all my mistakes, and in spite of not knowing what would happen next, I surrendered to God and said, "Here I am."

From that moment forward, I never looked back. I decided to put the corner piece of my life into the hands of the Cornerstone. My consistent motto became the phrase "whatever you have for me to do, I'm ready!" I really didn't know what I was saying at that point, but God knew, and I am grateful that He trusted me with my life's assignment and destiny.

At times as we travel through the unpaved roads of our past and the question marks of our identity, we are left with more questions than answers. We search for peace, and our search often leads us to discover that every fragmented piece of our lives and story will inevitably lead us back to God. But this truth still remains: the only One who can truly make you whole is God. The only One who can make sense out of the nonsense is God.

Why not pray this with me right now?

Here I am, God.
You can have every piece of me.

Pray this and declare these words until you feel transformation in your soul. When I made the decision to say yes, God began to reveal His plan for my life. Perhaps you have questions about your calling, or maybe you have unanswered questions stemming from a place of deep hurt. Most people do. I want you to know that every piece of your life can be used for God's purpose.

Since that August day in 2003, I have allowed God to mend the broken pieces of my life and show me my purpose. It is my hope that you will do the same. As painful as it may be for you to replay those events in your mind, it is a necessary part of discovering true healing and inner peace. My prayer is that you would find the shalom of God as you enter the place of peace that only He can provide. Trust God to cover every dark place in your life and to keep you during moments of deep loneliness. He did it for me, and He can do it for you. He will never leave you nor forsake you. My final prayer is that God would bring PEACE to your PIECES.

CHAPTER 7

CHAPTER

7

WHAT NOW?

FROM JAY

Many three-word phrases have the power to greatly affect the trajectory of a person's life. If you have been on the receiving end of one of these simple phrases, you know what I am talking about.

- "You are hired."
- "I am pregnant."
- "Paid in full."
- "You are fired."
- "He is dead."
- "You have cancer."
- "We are moving."
- "I am sorry."

Often these phrases will be followed by a two-word question: "What now?" She might kill me for writing this, but when my wife came home from her six-week checkup after giving birth to our second child and first son, she announced to me with a smile on her face, "I am pregnant!" You can probably guess my response after I got up off the floor. "What now?"

It was an August Sunday morning in 2001, and I was pastoring in LA (Lower Alabama). I was walking through the church, getting ready for the services that day, when my cell phone rang. Although it was not a number I recognized, I answered. My uncle proceeded to tell me that my dad had suffered a heart attack, but I honestly did not expect to hear the words that followed when he then announced, "He is dead." I fell to my knees in shock and wondered, "What now?"

I wonder if Isaiah felt some of those same emotions when he received the news that King Uzziah had died. Uzziah was appointed as king of Judah at the age of sixteen in 790 BC and reigned for fifty-two years. He was the son of King Amaziah and was one of the good kings of Judah. In 2 Chronicles 26:4 it says that he "did what was pleasing in the LORD's sight," just as his father had done. The next verse says that he sought God, and under Zechariah he learned to fear God. He was very intelligent and innovative, and in chapter twenty-six we discover that Judah prospered under his leadership, that the Philistines and Arabs were defeated, that he built fortified towers, and that the armies of Judah were strengthened and built up. He even invented weaponry that could be used from the walls of the city to attack approaching armies. Isaiah 6:1 says, "It was in the year King Uzziah died that I saw the Lord. He was sitting on a lofty throne, and the train of his robe filled the Temple." After fifty-two years of successful leadership in Judah, I would imagine that Isaiah might be asking the question, "What now?"

Half of America woke up angry Wednesday morning, November 9, 2016. Donald Trump, in a very surprising victory, had defeated Secretary of State Hillary Clinton the night before to become the forty-fifth President of the United States of America. Whether you are a Republican, Democrat, Independent, or you identify with no political party, you have probably had the thought at one time or another since that election, "What now?" Emotions have run high for everyone, the vitriol is escalating, racial division continues to be an issue, and unfortunately many people are more consumed with fixing blame rather than fixing the issues.

FROM DERRICK

After eight years of experiencing the country's first African American President, I felt a sense of pride as an African American. It seemed the dream Dr. King spoke of on August 28, 1963, during his memorable "I Have a Dream" speech, was possible. Perhaps the unity of black people, white people, and others from all nations could actually be achieved. We had come a long way from Jim Crow and other laws that prevented blacks from voting and now had a black man serving as President of the United States. A country that once voted to enslave African Americans voted to put one in the Oval Office. Though not every African American agreed with President Obama's polices, there was a strong sense of hope within the community. We were proud of the way he spoke, his intellect, and the way he represented the African American people. T-shirts had his face plastered on the front, and you could ride by homes of older people, sitting in rocking chairs on the front porch, wearing their President Obama hats. Overall, African Americans were happy they lived to see the first black president of our country. This had been a dream many blacks died fighting for and never got a chance to see. It confirmed the possibility that someone who looked like us could achieve the honor of being elected to the highest office in the land.

In 2016, as we neared the end of the Obama administration, most people resolved the country would be going in a different direction. Most African Americans were optimistic that Hillary Clinton would be the next president. Very few individuals in the African American community felt President Trump would actually win the election. Racial tension began building as we approached the 2016 election, but I don't think anyone was prepared for the conflict and strife that ensued on November 9, 2016. Anger and uncertainty infiltrated the black community after the election. Disunity and contention rose between the black and white communities. People I had been friends with for years began posting very hostile or belligerent comments on social media, and most African Americans were infuriated. It was one of the most divisive elections I had ever seen. I was struggling, personally, between my heart for the black community and my own convictions. I knew no matter what was ahead, the Lord would give me the wisdom to navigate His people through what was to come. I chose to stay committed to protecting the relationships I was building and contend for unity. Regardless of who our president was, I chose to believe God was the One in control.

FROM JAY

So what is our response and our responsibility in times like these? First of all, we are called to:

PRAY

All too often we underestimate the power of prayer. We claim to believe that prayer changes things and makes a difference, yet we do not practice what we believe. F.B. Meyer once said, "The greatest tragedy of life is not unanswered prayer but unoffered prayer."[12] Regardless of our political affiliation, the Bible calls for us to pray for our leaders. Paul writes in 1 Timothy 2:1-3 (NCV), "First, I tell you to pray for all people, asking God for what they need and being thankful to him. Pray for rulers and for all who have authority so that we can have quiet and peaceful lives full of worship and

---

12 https://www.goodreads.com/author/quotes/6446816.F_B_Meyer.

respect for God. This is good, and it pleases God our Savior." Paul wrote this during the reign of Nero, a Roman emperor who set Christians on fire and used them as human torches to light his gardens and banquet halls.

STAY ENGAGED

When things don't go our way, we have a tendency to disengage or to become discouraged and think, *What's the use?* When we disengage, we minimize God's ability to exponentially multiply the efforts and obedience of a few or of one.

Sir Nicholas Winton is responsible for rescuing 669 children from Nazi death camps. In 1938, this twenty-nine-year-old stockbroker from London cancelled his ski trip and spent his vacation in Prague with a friend, who told him of 150,000 people who had fled Czechoslovakia and were now in a refugee camp in Prague. Winton was drawn to the children, and he immediately began devising a way to get them to England by train. He set up a fake organization and negotiated with the British government, even though he had no experience dealing with refugees, to gain permission to begin receiving these children into England. He then found families who would take them in. On March 14, 1939, the first train carrying twenty children arrived. Between March and August that year six more trains would transport children, until the borders were closed on September 1, when Germany bombed Warsaw. A total of 669 children were saved. They settled in England, where they started a life, and now some 6,000 people are alive because of one man.[13] One man who could have just as easily said, "What's the use?"

God has always preserved a remnant of people who would be used to save a nation. In 2 Kings 19:31 we read this: "For a remnant of my people will spread out from Jerusalem, a group of survivors from Mount

---

13 "Sir Nicholas Winton," biography.com, https://www.biography.com/activist/sir-nicholas-winton.

Zion. The passionate commitment of the LORD of Heaven's Armies will make this happen!" Isaiah 65:9 says, "I will preserve a remnant of the people of Israel and of Judah to possess my land. Those I choose will inherit it, and my servants will live there."

I love the exploits of an ordinary man we read about in Judges 3:31: "After Ehud, Shamgar son of Anath rescued Israel. He once killed 600 Philistines with an ox goad." That's it. Seventeen words. One man, one great accomplishment. We know nothing else of him. What can we learn from Shamgar that can be applied to the struggles we are facing in America today?

1. **HE STARTED WHERE HE WAS.**

    He was living in a time and place when his life and property—and the lives and property of his family and countrymen—were at the mercy of Philistine thieves and thugs. Take a look at Judges 5:6-8:

    > *In the days of Shamgar son of Anath,*
    > *and in the days of Jael,*
    > *people avoided the main roads,*
    > *and travelers stayed on winding pathways.*
    > *There were few people left in the villages of Israel—*
    > *until Deborah arose as a mother for Israel.*
    > *When Israel chose new gods,*
    > *war erupted at the city gates.*
    > *Yet not a shield or spear could be seen*
    > *among forty thousand warriors in Israel!*

    He didn't wait for an army to form, or for friends to join him, or until weapons could be found. He knew he had a purpose, so he started where he was.

2. **HE USED WHAT HE HAD.**

An ox goad was not a weapon, but an instrument to herd oxen. One end had a sharp point and the other was flat like a paddle and was used to clear debris from the plow. In 1 Samuel 13:19 we read, "There were no blacksmiths in the land of Israel in those days. The Philistines wouldn't allow them for fear they would make swords and spears for the Hebrews." Moses had nothing but a shepherd's staff, but God used it to do miracles after asking Moses, "What do you have in your hand?" (Exodus 4:2). David only had a sling, but it was enough to kill Goliath. What do you have in your hand that God wants to use? A craft? An instrument? A skill? Money? Compassion?

3. **HE DID WHAT HE COULD DO.**

He did not make excuses. He made a difference. Just do what you can to make a difference, and do not minimize your contribution.

FROM DERRICK

I was newly married in 2007. Upon saying "I do," I instantly became a husband and new father. I was uncertain about my future and how to navigate thoughts of *not being good enough* for both roles. At the same time, my wife and I began helping Ronald and Kathy Robinson plant a church in Salisbury, North Carolina. We left everything we had to build that church and even moved in with them and their family. This decision altered the course of our lives.

In a matter of months, the church grew to nearly one hundred people. We were confident the Lord called us to ministry. The Robinsons also provided a safe place for us to grow in our relationship with Christ and in our marriage. Despite this growth, Shonda and I were really struggling financially while trying to raise two young kids, so we began seeking the Lord for direction.

On March 14, 2009, everything changed. Kathy Robinson, a lady who was affectionately known to many as "First Lady," died unexpectedly. Shonda and I were devastated. Kathy impacted our lives in a way that still yields fruit today. I started crying the moment I walked into the funeral service and continued until I left the building. I felt depleted. First Lady and I developed a special bond, and I didn't know how I would make it without her. I never felt a pain like that before. The memory of her body lying in the casket, dressed in her white garments with her hands tightly gripping her small, torn, green Bible, will remain etched in my mind forever.

A few months later the church closed, and Shonda and I were faced with finding a new church to attend and place to live. Pastor Darlene Allen, founder of The House of Refuge, delivered the eulogy for Kathy's homegoing celebration, as she was a relative of hers. After the funeral, I felt led to reach out to Bishop Allen and Pastor Allen to seek wisdom on what to do next. Shonda and I began to travel faithfully to the church they pastored in Greensboro to heal and find our footing. Eventually we made the decision to join The House of Refuge Deliverance Ministries.

In all the transition and turmoil, I lost my passion for church ministry. I just wanted to sit in services and spectate. But Bishop and Pastor Allen would not allow it. They saw something in me that I could not. Not long after we started attending, they approached Shonda and me about transitioning the church over to us, and we accepted.

Since assuming the pastoral role in 2016, Bishop and Pastor Allen have been our biggest cheerleaders and constant supporters. They have treated us as a son and daughter. They often say, "It's not about us, it's about God. This is God's vision." They have a genuine, God-given, love for Pastor Jay and The Refuge. As the campus grows and God continues to write the story of the merger, they gleam with a sense of pride. Rarely will a day pass before we talk, and they are always honoring of Pastor Jay and The Refuge. There would not be The Refuge Greensboro without the "Yes" of Bishop William and Pastor Darlene Allen. I'm grateful God allowed them to see the value in Shonda and me when we couldn't see it on ourselves. Without their faithful leading, we may not have taken this next step.

FROM JAY

THE EXTRA MILE

Jesus led an opposite Kingdom. And one of the principles He taught us was to do more than what is expected. This is countercultural to the mindset of today. Do not just do enough to fulfill some religious obligation. We are living in days where God will take our small contributions and multiply them to make a huge difference. What you do will stand out and showcase the heart of the Lord.

Jesus said in Matthew 5:13-16,

> "You are the salt of the earth. But what good is salt if it
> has lost its flavor? Can you make it salty again? It will
> be thrown out and trampled underfoot as worthless. You
> are the light of the world—like a city on a hilltop that
> cannot be hidden. No one lights a lamp and then puts
> it under a basket. Instead, a lamp is placed on a stand,
> where it gives light to everyone in the house. In the
> same way, let your good deeds shine out for all to see,
> so that everyone will praise your heavenly Father."

A few verses later we read,

"If a soldier demands that you carry his gear
for a mile, carry it two miles." (Matthew 5:41)

Roman soldiers could force citizens of Israel or any foreigner to carry their packs for a mile. Roman roads had mile markers similar to the mile markers we have today on Interstate highways, so it was easy to know where each mile started and ended. If someone refused to do it, he would be flogged. The Jews hated the Romans because they were Gentile foreigners running their country and they had to pay taxes to Caesar. Carrying a Roman soldier's heavy pack for a mile added to their hatred. When a Roman soldier told someone to carry his pack, the Jew would have to drop everything he was doing and go out of his way to obey the order.

Jesus tells His disciples to do more than what is expected. I believe it was in the second mile that life-changing conversations happened. It was in the second mile that a Roman soldier would begin to ask why they were doing what they were doing, and to ask about Jesus. When we are willing to go the second mile, we open the door for life-changing conversations to take place.

CHAPTER 8

CHAPTER

8

BARRIERS

FROM JAY

You have probably heard or read the story of pioneers who came to America some 350 years ago. This shipload of travelers landed on the northeast coast of America. The first year they established a town site. The next year they elected a town government. The third year the town government planned to build a road five miles westward into the wilderness. In the fourth year, the people tried to impeach their town government because they thought it was a waste of public funds to build a road five miles westward into a wilderness. Who needed to go there anyway? Here were people who had the vision to see three thousand miles across an ocean and overcome great hardships to get there. But in just a few years, they were not able to see even five miles out of town. They had lost their pioneering vision and their willingness to remove the barriers to progress.

With a clear vision of what our nation can become in Christ, no barrier or ocean of difficulty is too great. Without it, we rarely move beyond our current barriers. Helen Keller once said, "The only thing worse than being blind is having sight but no vision."[14] For years, The Refuge has faced many barriers. Starting in the basement of a house was far from glamorous and not what many would consider to be a wise church growth or church

---

14 https://www.brainyquote.com/quotes/helen_keller_383771.

planting strategy. For ten years, we met in two small warehouse buildings and shared our parking lot with a scrap metal facility. We often boasted that we were the only church in town with razor ribbon on our fence. We grew to four weekend services, added a campus twenty-five miles north, and added a campus in Brazil during those years. Yet we desperately needed a larger building.

We were finally able to purchase thirty acres of property on a main four-lane artery that ran through the county, and our desire was to begin building immediately. At the time, the church was seven years old, our finances were strong, and we were growing tremendously. But because we were less than ten years old, bank after bank refused to consider loaning us the millions of dollars needed to build a building. Many of them would not even meet with us. It seemed to be a huge barrier to progress, but with vision and faith we pressed through discouragement and God provided. On the day of our ten-year anniversary, we moved into our new state-of-the-art campus. Joel A. Barker says, "Vision without action is merely a dream. Action without vision just passes the time. Vision with action can change the world."[15]

When I announced the merger in September 2016, we were immediately faced with barriers, opposition, and reasons it would not work. (Derrick talks about those struggles in greater detail in chapter 9.) Barriers are nothing new when it comes to the spreading of the gospel and the advancement of God's agenda and message. Take, for example, the barriers Jonah faced when given a tough assignment by God to go to the city of Nineveh and preach. Jonah was a Jewish prophet who lived just north of Nazareth in Israel. Nineveh, the capital of Assyria and the reigning world power at the time, was some 500 miles away. It was located along the Tigris River near the modern city of Mosul, Iraq. Jonah did not like the city of Nineveh because he was aware of the Assyrians' reputation for being a cruel and wicked people who posed a great threat to the nation of Israel.

---

15 Joel A. Barker, *The Power of Vision* (Charthouse International Learning Corporation, 1991).

He knew that they had erected monuments to themselves, detailing the way they tortured and murdered anyone who opposed them. It is easy to understand Jonah's hesitation because of the likelihood that he, too, would be killed. He did the exact opposite of what the Lord ordered him to do, purchasing a ticket that took him as far away from his God-given task in Nineveh as possible.

Some of my earliest memories are of spending the night with my grandmother. She lived next door and died when I was five, but I can remember sitting on her bed at bedtime as she would share stories from the Bible with my brother and me. One of our favorites was the story of Jonah. You probably know the story well. His decision to run the opposite direction of Nineveh caused him to end up in the belly of a large fish, seaweed wrapped around his head, surrounded by half-digested, smelly fish in this pitch-black cavern far beneath the ocean's surface. From within the belly of this fish, Jonah prayed and repented for his disobedience and rebellion. And in Jonah 3:1-2 (NIV) we read a couple of my favorite verses in the Bible. It says, "Then the word of the LORD came to Jonah a second time: 'Go to the great city of Nineveh and proclaim to it the message I give you.'" I think that calls for a "praise break!" We have all blown it at times, just like Jonah. We have rebelled, refused to obey, run, resisted, recoiled, and rejected the assignment of God. Yet He is faithful to extend a second chance to us. And He did to Jonah as well. God caused the fish to have a severe case of indigestion and vomit Jonah up on the beach. Jonah heads towards Nineveh, vowing to obey God this time (hopefully after he had showered).

Once there, Jonah preached and a miracle took place. Jonah 3:5 says,

> The people of Nineveh believed God's message, and from the greatest to the least, they declared a fast and put on burlap to show their sorrow.

As Jonah preached to this wicked city of over 120,000 people, a city-wide transformation took place and people started repenting and crying out to God. As God saw that the Ninevites turned from their evil ways, He showed compassion and did not bring the destruction He had threatened. A city of 120,000 people was not only spared from the wrath of God, but everyone within that city was transformed by the power of God.

You might think Jonah would be excited about the transformation. Instead, he was angry. Jonah had had to overcome some barriers of distance, fear, and insecurity in order to fulfill God's assignment, but now we see another looming barrier inside of his heart that we also see in America today. Jonah was prejudiced towards the Assyrians. Removing barriers has a way of exposing deeper issues. Deep down Jonah was hoping that God would wipe them out. He carried hatred in his heart towards this enemy of Israel, people of a different race and ethnicity.

Maybe this book is exposing some things in your own heart, things that do not jive with the heart of God for all people. If so, are you willing to face those barriers and admit that they exist? Will you face the fear of moving beyond things you have been told that are now being exposed as false? Will you have the courage to sit down with someone of a different race and have an honest conversation? Will you listen to them and even admit if you have been wrong about some things?

As Jonah sat in the scorching sun pouting and processing his anger, God caused a plant to quickly sprout beside him that provided shade and temporary relief from the heat. However, as quickly as it had appeared, God caused it to die, further angering Jonah and exposing to Jonah that he cared more about his own comfort than he did the souls of people of a different race. The issue of racial division is centuries old in our nation, but I believe that with courage and an openness to giving God access to the deepest places of our hearts, it can be healed and eliminated.

FROM DERRICK

There is almost as much racial division in today's culture as existed in the sixties. The huge barrier is visible on Sundays in our sanctuaries, throughout the week at our corporate jobs, and in our everyday lives. The biggest difference is that it is more subtle, not as blatant with outward acts of hate but often disguised with hidden messages. In 2018, clothing company H&M came under fire for a children's ad that created an offensive narrative. At first glance one may not see an issue with the ad, which featured children in apparel appropriate for their age. The message was so subtle even my own daughter did not see it. The ad displayed two boys, a young white boy and a young black boy, standing side by side, both modeling hoodies, which is about where the similarities end. The hoodie worn by the white boy read: "Mangrove Jungle," and just below it the words "Survival Expert" with a picture of a tiger. The hoodie worn by the black boy read "Coolest Monkey in the Jungle."

People were outraged, but what is interesting is that the black boy's mom consented to it. Some saw it as just a shirt, just an ad. "What is there to be upset over?" Maybe you grew up reciting the phrase "Sticks and stones may break my bones, but words will never hurt me." We know there is no truth to that saying. Not only can words do great damage to a person, but words can divide and create barriers between us. For centuries African Americans were taunted and considered less valuable than animals. So the phrase "Coolest Monkey in the Jungle" on a shirt is extremely hurtful and offensive, especially to people who were not only called monkeys, but treated as such. And when compared to the Caucasian boy's shirt, which reads "Survival Expert" while displaying tigers and lions, known as hunters or as the kings of the jungle, this subtle message clearly supports the idea of the superiority of one race over the other. It is impossible to look at the photo and not cringe at the deeper meaning, and although it is subliminal and leaves the reader to create their own narrative, it contains a very demeaning and racist message and serves to erect more barriers.

The word *barrier* is defined as "something material that blocks or is intended to block passage, or a natural formation or structure that prevents or hinders movement or action."[16] It is interesting to consider that some of the most significant moves of God we read about in the Bible could have been prevented because of personal bias. Acts 10 provides a front-row seat to the dismantling of a barrier that was preventing the gospel from spreading beyond the Jews. Peter was in the town of Joppa, and one afternoon went up on a roof to pray. While praying, he had a vision of a large king-sized sheet being lowered from heaven, and inside the sheet were all sorts of animals, some of which would be forbidden for consumption by a Jewish person. Here is where the story takes an interesting twist. Acts 10:13-16 (NIV) reads,

> Then a voice told him, "Get up, Peter. Kill and eat."
> "Surely not, Lord!" Peter replied. "I have never eaten anything impure or unclean."
> The voice spoke to him a second time, "Do not call anything impure that God has made clean." This happened three times, and immediately the sheet was taken back to heaven.

Earlier in the chapter a Gentile man named Cornelius, a soldier in the Italian regiment whom the Bible describes as being devout, God-fearing, a man of prayer, and one who was very generous to the poor, also had a vision.

---

16 Merriam-Webster, s.v. "barrier," accessed September 6, 2020, https://www.merriam-webster.com/dictionary/barrier.

In this vision God told him to send men to the town of Joppa to invite a Jewish man named Simon Peter to his home. So while Peter was still on the roof trying to make sense of his vision, still resistant to the thought of doing anything that would defile him as a follower of the Law, the men arrived. Who doesn't love the slight rebellion of Peter because of the way it reminds us of ourselves? As much as he was full of faith, Peter wrestled with some real, internal issues that served as a potential barrier to the advancement of the gospel. We will come back to Acts 10 in a moment, but Peter's struggle might seem a little surprising when you consider what had happened on the Day of Pentecost in Acts 2.

Chances are that you are familiar with the events leading up to Acts 2, and how 120 individuals, from all different ethnicities, had gathered in an upper room in Jerusalem per the instructions of Jesus. The Bible makes a point of letting us know that they were there in complete unity, even though they were all very different. Peter was leading the charge of crying out to God, all while patiently awaiting the Spirit of God that was promised to come to empower, unify, and birth the Church. As promised, the Spirit came powerfully on those gathered in that upper room, and then soon spread into the streets of Jerusalem. We know from Scripture that the Holy Spirit fell not only on the Jews, but on every nation represented. Peter stepped up under the anointing of the Holy Spirit in Acts 2:14 and began preaching to the multiethnic gathering, resulting in 3,000 souls being added to the Church in one day! God used Peter in a mighty way, which raises the question, "Is it possible to be mightily used by God and be flawed?" And, "Is it possible to be used by God while having biased beliefs?"

To be *biased* means to be prejudiced in favor of or against one thing, person, or group compared with another, usually in a manner considered unfair. Could it be that we can sincerely love God and love His Church while still having favoritism in our hearts? Let's go back to Acts 10, where Peter is in a deep struggle between his religious beliefs and traditions of the Jewish law. The Law suggested that it was illegal for Peter to eat certain foods or even eat with Gentiles without becoming defiled or "unclean," according to Leviticus 11. Based on the Law, Peter was justified in his struggle. He felt that Jews were superior to Gentiles, so to entertain the thought that God would redeem Gentiles felt disloyal, almost a violation of everything he held true. God used food and "unclean" animals to expose a deeper issue in Peter's heart. He had a bias against people who did not look like him or hold to the same traditions.

Some people today live in communities whose residents feel that not just anyone should be allowed to live there. Others work at corporations that are inclusive to individuals who have certain degrees, have obtained a certain lifestyle, or drive certain cars. It is possible to obtain societal acceptance by means of wealth, possessions, or accomplishments and still suffer at the core of our souls. And not only do we suffer, but the advancement of the gospel suffers and becomes stagnant.

Cornelius loved God, was a devout believer and a man of great influence, yet there was still something missing from his life. It is interesting to consider that the one thing Cornelius needed is something that Peter had to offer. Cornelius was lacking Jesus. There have been many times throughout history that the removal of barriers in culture has come through someone we might have never expected.

Have you been calling the thing God is challenging you to do impure, or even questioning if it is from God? I am sure that when Pastor Jay met a black man in his early thirties who had nothing externally to offer, he could have rejected the vision of God because of opinion or discomfort. I was neither polished, nor did I possess anything of material value to bring to the table. He did not judge me by my exterior, nor did he reject me because of the color of my skin. He obeyed the voice of the Lord, looked at me as a person, and began pouring into and investing in my life. Although it was a struggle for him, Peter also obeyed God, and the next day he traveled with the men to the house of Cornelius in Caesarea. In Acts 10:34-36 (NIV) Peter shares this: "I now realize how true it is that God does not show favoritism but accepts from every nation the one who fears him and does what is right. You know the message God sent to the people of Israel, announcing the good news of peace through Jesus Christ, who is Lord of all."

THE GREENSBORO FOUR

The four young black college students who started the sit-ins on February 1, 1960, were charged with a deep conviction; a conviction that superseded their comfort. No longer could they stare injustice in the face and do nothing. There was an ugly, distinct barrier that needed to be broken in America. The Woolworth's department store located on 124 South Elm Street refused to serve African Americans at its lunch counters but allowed them to shop in their retail store. Joseph McNeil, Franklin McClain, Ezell Blair Jr., and David Richmond possessed the courage needed to break barriers. Some saw it as rebellion and an unruly breaking of the law. Yet for others this act was considered a courageous response to the injustice the country had been facing for years. The sit-in didn't begin at the counter, but rather in their hearts. These four students devised their plan in a dorm room of North Carolina Agricultural and Technical University, enlisting the help of a local white businessman named Ralph Johns, who was critical in helping put their plan into action. Contrary to popular belief, there were many whites who also hated and despised the injustice and mistreatment of blacks in the South.

On February 1, 1960, their plan was set into motion. McLain, McNeil, Blair Jr., and Richmond entered Woolworth's and sat at the whites-only lunch counter, where they were refused service. When asked to leave, they refused to give up their seats. Ralph Johns alerted the media to cover the events that were taking place. When the police arrived, there was little action because the protest was peaceful and the media was already present. The sit-in started on the first of February, and by the fifth, nearly 300 students had joined the protest. In the days to come, nearly 1,000 students would participate. The counters were filled with both black students and white students.

By March, some fifty-five cities and thirteen states were being impacted. The sit-in drew national news coverage and brought attention to the civil rights movement, and it had all been started by four black college students. Many people were arrested for trespassing and disorderly conduct, but the peaceful protests changed the South. During the summer while the students were away, Woolworth's quietly integrated, as did many other diners across the South. Geneva Tisdale, Susie Morrison, Anetha Jones, and Charles Best were workers at that Woolworth's in Greensboro and were the first blacks to be served once the diner integrated. Barriers that were broken down and removed in Greensboro changed not only the city of Greensboro, but our entire nation.[17]

What will your courage do? What will the nation write about one day that your church and you personally have done to help remove the racial barriers?

FROM JAY

Two of my greatest heroes, both now in heaven, are Dr. Martin Luther King Jr. and Rev. Billy Graham. Both left indelible marks on our nation, courageously battled against injustice, proclaimed the truths of God's Word,

---

17 Nadra Kareem Nittle, "How the Greensboro Four Sit-In Sparked a Movement," history.com, July 28, 2020, https://www.history.com/news/greensboro-four-sit-in-civil-rights.

and drew strength from their relationship with each other. Their friendship began in the 1950s and lasted until the untimely death of Dr. King on April 4, 1968. King is quoted as saying, "Had it not been for the ministry of my good friend Dr. Billy Graham, my work in the civil rights movement would not have been as successful as it has been."[18] In 1957, Billy Graham asked Dr. King to pray at his Madison Square Garden crusade in New York City, and he soon invited King to speak at a ministry retreat for the team of the Billy Graham Evangelistic Association and to help them understand more clearly the racial tensions and challenges in America.

On several occasions, due to his bold and unwavering stand against the mistreatment of blacks, Dr. King was arrested and thrown into jail. And it is a known fact that the person who posted bond for him on at least one of those occasions was Rev. Graham. What was it that forged such mutual respect, admiration, and close friendship between the two? I believe it stems from an incident in Chattanooga, Tennessee, in the Spring of 1953. Billy Graham walked into Warner Field House, the site of his upcoming crusade, and noticed white ropes sectioning off areas where whites would sit separately from blacks. He found the head usher and asked that the ropes be removed, but the usher refused. Billy Graham walked down off the platform and proceeded to remove the ropes himself. He then told the ushers who were threatening to put the barriers back up, "Either these ropes stay down or you can go on and have the revival without me."[19] From then on, Billy Graham put a policy in place that all of his crusades would be integrated and no barriers would be allowed to separate whites and blacks.

Now it is our turn to remove any barriers that still exist or have been allowed to remain in our nation, our communities, or even in our own hearts and minds. It took great courage for the Greensboro Four to do what they

---

18 Kate Shellnut, "What Is Billy Graham's Friendship with Martin Luther King Jr. Worth?" *Christianity Today*, February 23, 2018, https://www.christianitytoday.com/news/2018/february/billy-graham-martin-luther-king-jr-friendship-civil-rights.html.

19 "Billy Graham Holds First Integrated Crusade in Chattanooga, TN," The Association of Religion Data Archives, http://www.thearda.com/timeline/events/event_36.asp.

did. There was a price to pay for Dr. King and for Rev. Graham. Ralph Johns was criticized and misunderstood. Derrick and I have had to deal with barriers, criticism, and opinions from many as we have walked out this better narrative God is writing. Is it worth it? Without question. Are there still struggles? Same answer, and Derrick talks more about those struggles in the next chapter.

CHAPTER 9

9

STRUGGLES

On September 23, 2000, one of my all-time favorite movies was released, and it has continued to touch countless lives in the years since. *Remember the Titans* is a nonfiction film based on actual events that took place in Alexandria, Virginia, during 1971, when three public schools were forced to merge. Two predominantly white high schools consolidated with a predominantly black school to become T.C. Williams High School at a time when racial tension in America was at an all-time high. The movie highlights two men, Coach Bill Yoast and Coach Herman Boone.

Coach Yoast had been the head coach of T.C. Williams (the predominantly white school), and during the 1970 football season he led his team to the state championship. He was thought to have much more experience in coaching than Herman Boone. However, the school board elected to have Coach Boone lead the charge by making him head coach of the newly assembled football team as they integrated T.C. Williams High School. Coach Yoast became the assistant to a black man in a time when it wasn't popular for any white person to submit to anyone of color. Herman Boone was entrusted with carefully and strategically merging two different cultures. Not surprisingly, the merger between black and white schools presented major challenges. There were different styles of coaching, varying methods of discipline, and opposition from parents and coaches who didn't think this was a good idea. It was what some might call a "risky experiment." Yet despite the challenges, the two coaches were able to set their differences aside to lead the T.C. Williams Titans to a state championship that year. Coach Boone shared these words in a phone interview with The Washington Post:

> *No doubt, the beginning of our relationship was rocky. I didn't know Yoast. Yoast didn't know me. I knew that Hammond (where Yoast previously coached) had no black athletes and I didn't know if coach Yoast had anything to do with that. But we got to [training camp] and became roommates and found a way to talk to one another.*
>
> *I think that's the formula for race relations throughout the world. People have to learn to talk to one another. You have to learn to talk to that individual, and when you talk to that individual, you learn to trust that individual, and that's the greatest gift God gave to man.[20]*

Here is the thing about process; sometimes it takes longer to get something done, even after various people agree with it. The segregation of schools was rendered unconstitutional in 1954 (Brown vs. Board), but the schools in Alexandria didn't officially merge until 1971. Why did it take so long for certain places to desegregate? Jim Crow laws. The effects of Jim Crow laws were deeply rooted in the hearts of people. It wasn't as simple as combining schools together; there was an ideology embedded in the minds of people all across the country. To understand this, one needs to know what some of the Jim Crow laws were.

Jim Crow was the name of a set of laws that defined a racial caste system primarily operating in the southern border states. They were enacted during the 1870s and enforced until 1965. These were not just laws to most

---

20   Jacob Bogage, "Bill Yoast, assistant coach from T. C. Williams 'Remember the Titans' football team, dies at 94," *Washington Post*, May 24, 2019, https://www.washingtonpost.com/sports/2019/05/25/bill-yoast-assistant-coach-tc-williams-remember-titans-football-team-dies/.

people; in the Deep South, it became a way of life. The legal principal of "separate but equal" created a society in which African Americans were considered second-class citizens. Not only did politicians and community leaders hold this ideology about African Americans, but Christian leaders, ministers, and theologians taught that whites were the "chosen people," blacks were cursed to be servants, and racial segregation was supported by God.

In addition, there was a belief that innately, intellectually, and culturally, blacks were inferior to whites. Jim Crow laws served to legitimize anti-black racism. These laws undergirded certain beliefs that deepened the divide between the two races. Some of the laws consisted of a black male not being permitted to shake hands with a white man. If a white man shook a black man's hand, it implied the two were socially equal. This standard also applied to white women. There were other Jim Crow laws stating black individuals were not allowed to show affection toward one another in public, especially kissing, because it offended white individuals. If a black person rode in a car driven by a white person, the black person sat in the back seat or the back of the truck. They were not permitted to sit side-by-side in a vehicle. Black and white individuals couldn't attend the same barbershops, be buried near one another, sit at the same restaurant counters, and so on.

Though the country was changing, many people had a difficult time making the transition. The laws had been in effect for nearly one hundred years, and many struggled to adapt to a society in which all individuals were treated equally and allowed equal opportunities. In 1971, just six years after segregation laws ceased, people were still having trouble believing whites and blacks were equal. This is why it took the schools in the Alexandria, Virginia, school district so long to desegregate.

Forty-nine years ago blacks were still not considered equal. Considering my father is age fifty-seven, this truth is deeply emotional to me. I remember his stories of not having adequate education and the struggles he faced at South Rowan High School, located in North Carolina, during the late 70s and early 80s. I want to submit a thought for you to consider:

> ## Reconciliation will never be possible unless we begin to treat each other as equals.

RISKY EXPERIMENT

I will never forget the fall of 2016. Bishop and his wife, Pastor Allen, along with Shonda and myself, gathered together in Pastor Jay's office. He asked us a question that will remain etched in my memory forever. Pastor Jay and I had been meeting for over a year by this point, and we had developed a strong relationship. You could see his sensitivity and care as he sat up in his chair, uncrossed his legs, rubbed his head, and looked us dead in the eye before he spoke. "Do you want to date or do you want to be married?" he asked. To be honest, I didn't completely know what being married to The Refuge would look like, but I knew we didn't want to date. He asked us to pray about it and shared what being married versus dating looked like. Dating meant we could stay in connection and he would continue to mentor me as my pastor and support our leaders as he had been, but there wouldn't be as deep of a relationship as in a marriage.

If we married, we would take on the same name, systems, processes, culture, and DNA of The Refuge. We would combine our resources, and our building would become an extension of The Refuge. The House of Refuge Deliverance Ministries name would completely go away, and we would become a campus of The Refuge. Pastor Jay would become the lead pastor, and Shonda and I would become campus pastors. It also meant I would be a part of the staff of The Refuge, and my wife would be tasked with the responsibility of helping to navigate this transition.

At that time, Shonda and I had already been married for nine years, and we had a "blended family," as some may call it. We remembered how difficult the first few years of our marriage were and the challenges we faced as we were trying to navigate becoming one family. Both of us knew that as great as we felt about becoming a campus of The Refuge, there would be obstacles and challenges. I mean, this was risky, not just for us, but also for Pastor Jay and The Refuge. No one in the room made light of the question posed. It weighed heavily on each of us as we contemplated what a marriage of the two churches would look like.

The moment we left the room, my mind began racing. I reflected on when Shonda and I were first married and how we still had to get to know each other. As much as we both loved one another, we had to figure out how our lives would come together. It would be the same way with the two churches. Like any marriage, you have the honeymoon phase where you are head-over-heels in love with each other. You look at one another and you can't help but blush. Then, there are times when you walk into the bathroom and the last bit of toothpaste is squeezed or someone left the toilet seat up and you think, *what did I get myself into?* I had not even assumed the position as lead pastor of The House of Refuge. *Am I rushing this decision? Do we need to take this slower? I mean, what if it doesn't work?* All of these questions began to run through my mind. I was already faced with the struggle of taking over a very traditional church. I didn't have the trust of the members yet, and I was a brand-new pastor. Now I questioned if God was asking me to merge our churches at all. There were so many times when I went back and forth wrestling with the decision. I told God it felt like I'd be giving up a lot. It wasn't so much about the name or even the building—I questioned if I would lose my identity. Not only would I become a campus pastor, but I would no longer be responsible for preaching and preparing my own sermons. I wouldn't be casting my vision and my own ideas. *Would it be worth it?*

I had to ask myself the question, *Can you submit to another man's vision and serve it as your own?* For me, it wasn't about the color of his skin as much as it was the freedom I would have and what I would be giving up. So many people asked me, "Are you sure you want to do this? Black people were enslaved for years, and you want to have a white man as your pastor?" This was said by people I trusted. I valued their opinions. They began to call me an Uncle Tom and said I was the token black guy. *What if they were right?* I remember telling Shonda, "I don't think I can do this." As time passed, I began to feel God reassure me that He had me. I didn't understand what He was doing or even why He was allowing me to do it. I just knew it was bigger than me. Every time a divisive thought or comment was made, the Lord sent random confirmation through someone to let us know this merger was orchestrated by God.

CULTURAL DIFFERENCES

As we neared November, there were a series of meetings held between Bishop, Pastor Allen, and myself concerning what we felt the Lord was asking us to do in terms of merging the churches. Once we made the decision to merge, we held a meeting with the members of The House of Refuge Deliverance Ministries. I will never forget the moment we broke the news to our church that we would be joining The Refuge as a campus. Silence hushed over the room. Most of the people were in agreement, but there were a few who really struggled with the news. One lady approached me after the meeting and asked, "Pastor, is there not a black church we can merge with?" There were already some who felt as though I was unqualified to lead the church, and now there were others who thought we had really lost our minds. Questions and comments came flooding in. "Merger? What is that? So, you won't be our pastor?"

A sequence of meetings followed. Pastor Jay brought key pastors and leaders to the Greensboro Campus to help us navigate through the transition. Pastor Jay gave us the date he felt I should transition into the role of Lead Pastor of The House of Refuge, as well as the timeline our campuses would officially merge. He felt it was very important that I have an opportunity to establish my leadership in this new role prior to merging. So, in June of 2016 Pastor Jay came to Greensboro and preached my installment service. Pastor Jay, along with Bishop and Pastor Allen, laid hands on me and prayed as they passed the baton as the senior pastor of the church. After twenty years of pastoring, Bishop and Pastor Allen's children struggled with their parents no longer being the senior pastors, wondering what their parents' new roles would be. Equally, members who helped found the church grappled with how their positions would change with a new pastor and the reality of becoming an entirely different church. *How would the transition be made?* There were so many questions to be answered, and the sense of urgency became too much to bear. We continued to hold countless individual meetings with the church members and Pastor Jay in preparation of the merger announcement to come in September of that same year.

Another hardship to navigate was the cultural differences; not just in race, but in style and tradition. Our church service styles were completely different. Throughout the history of the black church, there have been three monumental shifts in culture that have affected our style of worship. The first was the introduction of women in ministry, led by Ida B. Wells. This shift promoted opportunities for missionary societies, Sunday school teaching, conferences, and conventions centered around the empowerment of women. Programs that assisted with meeting the needs of communities were started by women.

Another cultural shift was the civil rights movement. During the height of the civil rights movement, the black church offered cultural direction and political commentary in an era that was often clouded with social injustice. The black church became known for its social justice and political leadership, while the white church in general focused more internally on personal growth and discipleship.

The Great Migration between 1916 and 1970, the time when African Americans moved from rural areas to urban areas, also affected the church. The Northern white church initially serviced freed slaves and those migrating north by educating them and helping them find a trade and a place in a society that didn't include them. While this assistance was needed, it also greatly influenced the worship styles of African Americans in the north. Black Northerners expressed worship subtly, with thought and poise. The Southern black church uses more of a folklore presentation of sermons and exuberant expression of worship. There became a distinction between the two cultures, with the Northern shunning the Southern church and their expressive notions.

The term "black church" derives from the academic category of the "Negro Church" titled by Dr. W. E. B. Du Bios. Most often, black churches are classified by one category, but in reality they are quite diverse institutions, each having their own historical foundations. There are seven major denominations closely associated with the black church: The National Baptist Convention, National Baptist Convention of America, Progressive National Convention, African Methodist Episcopal Church, African Methodist Episcopal Zion Church, Christian Methodist Episcopal Church, and Church of God in Christ. Some African American religious roots date back to the years of slavery when some slaves were permitted to sit in the back of the white church their slave master attended. The sermons often emphasized the importance of obedience, service, and loyalty. Ministers would quote Paul's admonition—"Slaves, obey your masters"—

during weekly services. This type of teaching led us to develop the tradition of pleading to God for freedom, like the Hebrew slaves who were rescued out of Egypt and written about in Exodus. The narrative shared in the black church was often about the hope of redemption. The black church has been the pinnacle of and the epicenter for the African American existence in America, with their communities functioning as a place of encouragement and understanding in the midst of suffering.

The black church has been known for its traditions and how we conduct services. One tradition, widely attended and accepted across multiple African American denominations, is Watch Night. The tradition of Watch Night first began in the Moravian church around the eighteenth century as a vigil to express a time of reflection on the past year and usher in the year to come. On December 31, 1862, Watch Night was redefined by the black church as slaves stayed up all night, gathered in homes and churches, to pray over the pending signing of the Emancipation Proclamation which declared all slaves legally free. Throughout the years, Watch Night has transformed beyond its origin, changing much of its traditional meaning into a time of celebration at the beginning of the New Year. We come together to thank the Lord for His blessings of the past year and for the year to come.[21] The black church is a complex entity with a foundation in trial and triumph, bondage and freedom, which became the foundation for a people who had nothing to build from.

Our expression of worship is relevant to the oppression from which we've been delivered. A traditional way to celebrate God's Word and blessing requires a corporate jubilee termed a "praise break." In some black churches, there is also a moment when the organist and musicians play behind the pastor as he reaches a climactic point of the message. We call this "the close." Many African American churches are very expressive in gratitude toward God. So much so, that you are liable to see someone take off in a

21 "What Watch Night Really Means for People of Faith," beliefnet.com, https://www.beliefnet.com/faiths/christianity/articles/what-watch-night-really-means-for-people-of-faith.aspx.

full sprint around the church under the unction of the Holy Spirit. In many white churches, during worship hands are lifted, but it's typically quieter. There is no "Amen Corner" from which people shout "Hallelujah" or "Say it, pastor" when the Word is being taught. White congregations tend to kneel at the altars, and you can hear a pin drop while the pastor is preaching.

The worship portion of the service can be totally different as well. The black church has five to six singers singing in a three-part harmony accompanied by various instruments playing a plethora of melodies. In the white church, the singers sing in unison with the keyboardist playing softly in a dimly lit auditorium.

Then, there is the coffee shop that has been recently added to many new, predominantly white churches. My grandmother would die if she saw me drinking coffee in the sanctuary! We weren't allowed to eat or drink in the sanctuary out of respect for God's house. Other similar reverences affected things we did and didn't do in the sanctuary. For instance, we wouldn't talk during service, chew gum, or walk during prayer, and we always stood for the reading of the Word out of respect for God and lasting traditions.

The style of dress and preaching is also different. Worship leaders in white churches often don ripped jeans and chelsea boots, while traditional black churches desire to honor God by wearing our best outfits. Communication styles vary between teaching and preaching. In the black church, the Word is preached with much charisma and vibrato, causing the preacher to sometimes inflate his voice as he delivers the message to his audience.

Though I noted many of these differences between The House of Refuge and The Refuge, one thing was evidently the same: The Spirit of God. I felt it every time I walked into The Refuge. It didn't matter how different the structure or style of the building was or how different the services were, I'll never forget the presence I felt during the first service I attended. I was wrecked. I couldn't stop weeping. I felt God move in such a strong way.

There were so many reasons why this merger shouldn't work, and we had every excuse to say let's just stay in our comfort zones and stick to what we have always done. That's the easy way out. But we want revival, and

Pastor Jay and I truly believe the prerequisite for revival is unity. This doesn't mean everything will be a struggle, but there will be some challenges we will have to work through together. One of the core values of The Refuge states that we courageously deal with conflict in a biblical manner, fiercely protect unity, and place a high value on relationships (James 1:2-3, 1 Peter 3:8-9, 1 Corinthians 13:8, Romans 16:7). We also make every effort to keep the unity of the Spirit through the bond of peace (Ephesians 4:3). It requires effort to be intentional about these matters. There have been times of anger and frustration as we have found our stride. But it's a marriage. I have been angry and upset with my wife, but I didn't ask for a divorce or leave because we hit a rough patch. We made vows, and our commitment to each other is what it means to be married.

Racism has been one of the great sins of our nation. I am not unaware of the challenges, systems, and thoughts of people who do not think the same way I do. I just refuse to be silent. Just because I've merged a black church with a white church, I'm not exempt from being racially profiled or judged by the color of my skin. It also doesn't protect me from experiencing injustices toward black and brown people. What I can't allow myself to do is judge a group of people because of one person's perspective. I remember a day I traveled to the Kannapolis campus of The Refuge for our monthly staff meeting. I drove through a town called China Grove that is between Salisbury and Kannapolis. At the time, I was driving a Hyundai Genesis. It had factory tint and low-profile tires. As I neared a stoplight, I saw a cop approaching me through my rearview mirror. I knew I hadn't been speeding, so I wondered why lights were flashing behind me. As he pulled me over, a sense of fear ran through my body. I was terrified. As he walked up to my driver-side window, he asked for my license and registration. I trembled as I pulled them out of my pocket. I kindly asked the white officer why he pulled me over. He couldn't tell me. At that moment, I didn't know if I would have a chance to make it home to my wife or children. I was scared for my life, and no one should ever have to feel that way. As my hands began to tremble, he saw the look in my eyes and let me go. No ticket. No warning. No explanation. Not one word.

I arrived at the office with so many emotions running through me. I was furious. I began to share my experience with Pastor Jay, and he showed compassion for me. He didn't tell me it wasn't true or that profiling doesn't exist. He listened. I couldn't take my experience with the officer out on him, because he didn't do it. He also did not try to convince me it never happened. Unity is not the absence of conflict or misunderstanding, it is our ability to acknowledge there are some things in this country that affect one group of people more than they do others. We must be willing to listen to one another and seek understanding of struggles they face. That doesn't mean that we can't love our own race and embrace another one at the same time. It means we acknowledge that there are real challenges and differences we have to address but remain unified.

Pastor Jay and I will admit we don't always see things the same way or have all the answers. Much like Herman Boone and Bill Yoast, we have different styles of leadership, methods of handling situations, and ways we view things, but what makes us the same is the Spirit of God. Eventually, Herman and Bill had to rely on their strengths and not focus on their weaknesses. They had to choose to put the priority on unifying the team. Instead of partnering with the deception of the enemy, the team began to play together. The struggles and challenges have helped Pastor Jay and me forge our relationship. We are following the leading of the Holy Spirit as He helps us navigate through what He has called us to. At every turn, we are learning more about each other and the culture of each church and embracing the similarities and differences.

OVERCOMING THE STRUGGLES

A *kairos* moment is defined as a propitious time for decision or action. Scholars and writers would call a kairos moment the appointed time in the purpose of God. What happened when the merger became official on November 6, 2016, couldn't have been planned; we are not that smart, nor are we that wise. When we made the announcement of the merger, I felt the wind of God blow and propel this union to the forefront of our nation in ways that defied human reason. You could tell this was a priority to God and the purpose of God was being revealed. God was using our story to unify a nation.

Many events leading up to the merger would have been impossible for a man to manufacture. Pastor Jay and I have depended on the wisdom of God to lead us through very challenging times. Multiple shootings occurred across the nation, and several took place in our own backyard—one of which is the Keith Lamont Scott shooting that occurred in Charlotte. Pastor Jay was consistent in reaching out to me, throughout these times, to ask how our church was feeling and how I was doing. When we officially announced the merger on September 22, 2016, the crowd at the Kannapolis campus erupted with applause. But there were still feelings of anxiety amongst the congregation in Greensboro. With so much turmoil going on around us, there was a general sense of unease.

True courage and strength are built in times of adversity. The church was uneasy after the merger, and we knew people were looking to us to show them how to overcome these racial and cultural challenges within the church and surrounding communities. They tuned in to see how we would address the elephants of race, and even politics, in the room. We had to establish boundaries. Some things were sensitive topics, so we chose to focus our attention on building relationships and our understanding of

Scripture, while allowing the Holy Spirit to knit our hearts together. When something bothered me, I didn't take my feelings to social media or to other members of the church. I went to Pastor Jay to discuss them in private. No matter how tough the conversation was, he never judged me. He listened.

In our church community, people were uncertain about the days to come. Many people came to me asking what our plan was for the church. There was an expectation from some of the people within our church for diversity to occur overnight. Some also assumed we would morph our building and systems in a matter of days of becoming The Refuge. Both of these ideas were unrealistic. Our campus is located on the eastern side of Greensboro in one of the roughest parts of the city. If I'm honest, in my own mind, I struggled with the possibility of a person of any other ethnicity driving to that side of town to come to our services. So I did the only thing I knew to do: I prayed.

I also made a lot of mistakes during this process. There was no manual on how to do this. We didn't have a blueprint of anyone who had done anything remotely close to what we were doing. Most of our learning came through trial and error. We started with subtle changes, like on-boarding the members of The House of Refuge to members of The Refuge. Let's just say, I experienced major pushback. Some of the members felt as though they should have been grandfathered into The Refuge because of the merger. We changed out the signage, added flags, and did some minor upgrades to change the look of the building. That went over better than I thought, and we were beginning to make progress. We had to be strategic in introducing processes and ideas to the campus slowly. We knew we had heard God, but that didn't mean it was going to be an easy transition. In the first year, some people chose to leave. Between my transition to campus pastor and the merger, some people felt this was not something they were called to be a part of. There were moments when I battled discouragement and even struggled with depression. I didn't know fully what I was getting myself into. I kept my priority and focus on Jesus and sought counsel from trusted voices who truly believed in what we were doing.

It's been four years since the initial merger, and we have learned a lot. We learned how to set healthy boundaries. We listened to each other and have worked hard at building trust. We found out what would and wouldn't work for us. We initially thought it would be good to send the Sunday morning message from Kannapolis via video to our Greensboro Campus. We later found out it was received better if I preached the messages live. We also knew it would be necessary for Pastor Jay to speak at the campus and preach there periodically to ensure the campus felt connected. Pastor Jay began hosting revival services at the start of every year called Launch. All of our campuses are invited to come together for a time of worship and prayer to kickstart the year. This has helped to unify us as one church. We are becoming more intentional with our video announcements and also the diversity of singers and band members leading on Sundays. Our Greensboro worship leaders travel to Kannapolis monthly to lead worship, as well. We have annual staff retreats where our entire team goes away to seek the face of God and spend time building relationships. It is not perfect. We are always finding more things we can do to improve. But we are far from where we were in 2016, and I believe the best is yet to come. I believe that when we focus on our strengths, our struggles begin to get less important. We desire to do our part in our nation and in our church to keep racial reconciliation as a priority because it's a priority to God.

In the story of *Remember the Titans*, in just one year the two coaches were able to overcome challenges and win the state championship. I only wish we could do what those two coaches were able to do in one year. We are realistic, and we know it will take time. In the moment of victory both coach Boone and Yoast shared, it wasn't about a black coach or white coach winning—it was about the team. That is what it is all about for Pastor Jay and me. It is about building a church that will glorify God. We are still navigating through the challenges of becoming a multiethnic family and not just multicultural, because there is a difference. We don't want one culture of ethnicity to be superior to the other. We are believers celebrating the differences and unique things that make us beautiful.

You know the saying, "Rome wasn't built in a day"? Well, neither will this church. It takes time. But hey! We aren't dating. We are married, so we have time to grow together. I don't believe Jesus is coming back for a white church or a black church. He is coming back for His unified bride who loves Him and desires to please Him. We desire to please Him. There has been more effort to listen to the challenges in black communities as well as the systems and teachings from other leaders of different ethnicities to help us to become what God has designed His bride to be. No matter the challenges ahead of us, we are committed to reconciliation.

CHAPTER

10

10

SHAPING CULTURE

FROM DERRICK

Growing up in the South, I heard the stories of racism and even had some personal experiences, but nothing could have prepared me for two videos that went viral in May of 2020. One was of a young black man by the name of Ahmaud Aubery, and the other was of the public murder of George Floyd. The country watched the disturbing footage of Ahmaud being chased and gunned down by three white men while on a run in the Satilla Shores neighborhood in Brunswick, Georgia. We also watched as George Floyd was murdered on a sidewalk in Minneapolis, Minnesota, by an officer whose knee was pressed into his neck. He struggled to breathe and pleaded for his life as the officer continued to press his knee into George's neck, cutting off his air supply, for 8 minutes and 46 seconds. Other officers watched and did nothing.

Watching these videos made me angry. I was upset, and the trauma consumed me. Like many who watched these audacious and senseless murders, questions flooded my mind: How could they let this happen? Why do things like this keep happening? But then, it seemed as though a miracle began unfolding as millions of others who watched had the same or similar sentiments. Something was beginning to shift. People—including white people—were finally tired of seeing innocent men and women being brutally murdered with no positive outcomes and often no convictions.

This is a book about unity. It is our story of how we found and fought for it, and how we desire to bring hope to a nation that is fractured and hurting. But it is important for you to know that even for us, it was never simple. Even in a success story like ours, there are challenges. We will talk more about that in a moment.

FROM JAY

THE SAGA OF JOHN

John faced some legitimate challenges in his life. He boarded a ship bound for England, his home, full of bitterness, discouraged, with his tail tucked between his legs. His very first pastorate had ended after three years in utter failure. John had grown up in a home with eighteen siblings, raised by godly Anglican parents, Sam and Susanna, who taught him to fear the Lord and love the Word. He felt called to ministry, studied at Oxford, and upon graduating received a call to pastor British colonists in Savannah, Georgia.

On his way to America in October of 1735, a fierce storm arose, threatening to destroy the ship. Many passengers, including John, who ironically served as the ship's chaplain, feared for their lives. But John noticed a group of German Moravians, on their way to America to preach to Native Americans, who possessed a calmness that allowed them to sing throughout the constant battering of the winds and waves and the torrents of rain. After the storm passed, John asked the leader of the Moravians how they were able to remain so calm, to which the leader asked, "Do you have faith in Christ?" John responded affirmatively, but somehow felt an emptiness to his words even as he spoke them. That emptiness would continue to gnaw at his soul.

Upon his return to England three years later, John would join a Christian society led by Moravians. It was in one of these prayer settings, on May 24, 1738, that John would feel his "heart strangely warmed," leading to what some refer to as John's evangelical conversion. With a new fire and passion, John began preaching and discipling people across England, forming groups of people to study God's Word who would later be known as Methodists. It could be argued that were it not for the Moravians, John likely would have quit the ministry. But because of division and disunity, their encounter with John almost never happened.[22]

A new community of believers began forming under the leadership of a young twenty-seven-year-old aristocrat named Count Zinzendorf in 1722. They named their community Herrnhut, and within five years the community had grown to around three hundred people. But rather than being known for their passion for God's Word and prayer, they were characterized by dissension, fighting, and an inability to get along with each other. Count Zinzendorf and others made a covenant to labor in prayer for revival as a hopeful antidote for disunity, and revival indeed came on May 12, 1727. On August 13 of that year, twenty-four men and twenty-four women committed to pray one hour each day, covering each hour of every day of the week with two people per hour. This commitment on their part launched a 24/7, 365-days-a-year prayer movement that would last for the next 100 years! And out of that prayer movement missionaries were sent around the world to preach the gospel. Among them was a group of people who boarded a ship in 1735 bound for America who would meet a young pastor named John Wesley.[23]

---

22 "John Wesley, Methodical Pietist," *Christian History*, https://www.christianitytoday.com/history/people/denominationalfounders/john-wesley.html

23 "Moravians at Herrnhut," *Christianity.com*, https://www.christianity.com/church/church-history/timeline/1701-1800/moravians-at-herrnhut-11630204.html. See also "August 13th services," Home Moravian Church, https://www.homemoravian.org/index.php/who-we/our-worship/august-13th-services/.

Prayer and unity are prerequisites for revival. In Acts 2, a diverse group of 120 people packed into a second-floor room in Jerusalem with rather vague instructions from Jesus to "tarry there" in prayer. But for how long? With what expectations? Their world was a mess, divided and confused, and Jesus hadn't given them much to go on. What they thought was going to happen took a one-eighty, leaving them reeling like a heavyweight MMA fighter who didn't see the right hook coming. They thought Jesus would deliver them from Roman oppression by establishing a new political order in the form of a kingdom where He would put the Romans in their rightful place and all of them would take positions of prominence. Now, their new king had been killed, and they were huddled together in prayer.

As I write this chapter, our world finds itself in an unprecedented season, dealing with a pandemic, economic collapse, racial division, anarchist groups, rioting, death, fear, political unrest, and the shutdown of churches, schools, and businesses. We have become uncomfortably familiar with words that, prior to 2020, we never knew or only rarely heard—words and phrases like pandemic, social distancing, herd immunity, droplet transmission, asymptomatic, flattening the curve, coronavirus, shelter-in-place, PPE, and quarantine. We hear things like "defunding the police" or "CHOP zones" or "Antifa," and are bombarded daily by the media with charts, statistics, Op-Eds, White House briefings, and updates.

Are there parallels we can draw and dots we can connect from what gushed out of that upper room in Jerusalem and changed the known world at that time, to what our response should be now? In the book of 1 Chronicles, we read of 200 soldiers known as the Sons of Issachar: "From the tribe of Issachar, there were 200 leaders of the tribe with their relatives. All these men understood the signs of the times and knew the best course for Israel to take" (1 Chronicles 12:32). The days of anemic, wimpy, preschool fun-and-games Christianity are over. We need warriors, men and women who will press their ear close to the heart of Jesus, feel His heartbeat, understand the unique times in which we live, and get the strategy of heaven for our dysfunctional, broken, messed-up world.

FROM DERRICK

TOUGH QUESTIONS

Pastor Jay and I recently had a challenging conversation. At one of our regular meetings, I asked him a question that I have asked him before: "When we look at our church and our world, is the field equal?" Pastor Jay doesn't blink when I ask those type of questions. I think by now he probably knows they are coming. He knows that these are questions I think about, especially now, with everything that our nation has been experiencing. What would a fair America look like? What would it be like to live in a country that treats everyone the same, that gives the same chances to people of all different skin colors?

There's often a misconception in white America that when we talk about equality, African Americans are looking for handouts. We're not. What we want is an equal playing field. We just want the same experiences and opportunities we see available to other ethnicities. There are so many disparities that black communities face that other communities do not, like mass incarceration, police brutality, the black income gap, and gaps in healthcare. And this inequality exists in the church, too. "I'm not looking for a handout," I told Pastor Jay. "I'm just looking for a fair race." He didn't dismiss me or my concerns or try to override them by endeavoring to find the perfect words. He just listened.

I could tell Pastor Jay took in every word I said with extreme compassion and care. As we concluded our meeting, we hugged, as we do at the end of most of our meetings. I thanked him for listening. As is often the case with great meetings, we walked away with more questions. We know we do not have all the answers to what a healed America, free of racism, looks like. I know what I feel it should look like, which is a world that embraces differences and one that listens to and appreciates the value of every ethnicity. It is a world that places a value on building relationships instead of sectioning people off by skin color; a world that makes Jesus the priority. What does a healed America look like to you? What are you doing to achieve it?

FROM JAY

Prayer and unity. Can it be that simple? Maybe, but I believe action is also required. There is an entire book in the Bible based on the actions of God's people called Acts of the Apostles. However, the foundation for any action has to be prayer and unity. Otherwise, we become dependent on our own abilities and begin trusting the god of Self more than the One True God. Our actions independent of the power of the Spirit can lead to counterproductive results that actually end up working against the very things we are trying to accomplish. For example, contrast the lives and accomplishments of Malcolm X and Dr. Martin Luther King Jr. One was driven by anger and ambition, the other by a dream to see the prayer of John 17 fulfilled. One was fueled by the concept of man-produced revolution, the other by the concept of God-produced reformation. It was clear that Dr. King's was a life bathed in prayer and operating in the strength of the Holy Spirit. As a result, the fruit of his actions, aided by the Principle of Outward Impact, is still having a positive effect on culture today.

Action is essential. I believe there is a place for protests and that good can result from them. But if the protests are not birthed from the place of prayer and in unity with the Spirit, people may be pushed to a place of rebellion, and any resulting change will be temporary because it is built on a foundation of human effort rather than the Spirit of God. I believe God desires to shake our nation to its foundation and birth a movement of prayer that will rally people around His presence, releasing a unified cry for true revival.

FROM DERRICK

A SPREADING FIRE

In 2019, I visited The International Civil Rights Center and Museum in Greensboro, North Carolina, with Pastor Jay and some staff members from The Refuge. We were led through some of the history of our nation by a middle-aged female African American tour guide with gray locks. She made a deep impression on me as she shared the brutal history of our nation, holding me captive at every word with her knowledge and eloquent presentation. I was struck with a deep feeling of pain as I toured the dark halls of the museum, staring at walls filled with pictures of blacks and whites who were instrumental in helping to shape our country. I felt like I was experiencing every moment as it was happening. Their contributions to the history of our culture and their sacrifices are priceless and so courageous.

At one point in the tour, our attention was directed to an old Coca-Cola machine from decades past. One side of the drink machine, intended for white customers, lists the price of a Coke as five cents. The other side of the machine, once separated by a wall, was for "colored" customers. The price of a Coke on this side was ten cents. During our tour, I saw pictures and videos of police officers with dogs and fire hoses they used to spray black men and women until they fell helplessly to the ground, their skin ripped off their bodies. I felt the weight of this experience in a way that I am still processing. I struggled to hold back the tears and found myself struggling to find even a glimpse of hope.

As the tour was coming to an end, our tour guide instructed us to gather around a huge round table. On the table was a large map of the United States filled with highlighted cities that helped end segregation in the South. She showed us how the sit-in in 1960 at that very location, formerly a Woolworth's Department Store, spread from Greensboro, North Carolina, all throughout the South. As she spoke, something significant happened to me. I heard the still, small voice of God saying, "Revival will spread like this across our nation again, and in the nations of the world." For the past few years, I had felt that stir of revival, not in a sense of mere services and tent revivals but in the sense of the presence of God captivating our hearts again. I noticed that my prayers had become stronger in my private time with God. I felt that 2020 would be the beginning of a shift in culture, that something significant was about to take place in our world.

Our nation was crying out, and the sin of racism and injustice was rearing its ugly head once again. The cry for justice and equality was screaming to be heard. People had had enough, and people from all walks of life, ethnicities, and religious beliefs began to rally together. Riots and protests began. The unheard, those of us used to being told to "get over it already"— the most insensitive thing you can say to people who have experienced trauma—were being heard, seen, and joined. There it was: a shift, the beginnings of revival.

FROM JAY

SOUND OF REVIVAL

Each Sunday I meet with our pastors for prayer to start the day. On August 9, 2020, we gathered in my office at 8:00 a.m. I said to them, "There is something different about today." We began praying, and simultaneously our worship team was rehearsing an original song, debuting that day, called "Sound of Revival." As they sang and as we prayed, the building literally shook! Just ninety-five miles away, in Sparta, North Carolina, a 5.1 magnitude earthquake hit, felt as far away as Atlanta, Georgia, and places in northern Alabama. I immediately knew that this natural event paralleled what was going on in the Spirit realm. As the earth's plates were shifting, there was a shift taking place in the work of the Spirit.

The culture of prayer is well established at The Refuge. We do not depend on cool decor, LED walls, great coffee, leather couches, or a tattooed staff to change anyone's life. We know and live by the mantra that nothing of lasting value happens without prayer. Since our earliest days, we have held all-night prayer meetings called Nightwatch. We have multiple prayer meetings that take place throughout the week. I believe that there is a unique anointing for prayer on African Americans. They are some of the most faithful in prayer, and some of the most passionate prayers. I love to be in settings where they are participating in or leading prayer.

FROM DERRICK

I can hear the stirrings and the sound of revival, but I know it is going to take a lot to bring about the change we need. And I believe that the way we will see and experience lasting change is through prayer. Prayer is one of the most essential ways we can invite God into our lives. But prayer cannot just be about the things we want. We must be willing to incorporate repentance, admission, humility, and a desire to change. We can never change the world if we do not first change ourselves. I was raised around praying individuals who did not have much in terms of material possessions. But what they did have was a life committed to prayer and intercession.

I can remember hearing and seeing my grandmothers pray. My fondest memory of my dad's mother, Ella Odessa Bost, was of her being on her knees when we came in from playing in the neighborhood. As we walked in the house, we would hear this bellowing sound coming from her room that would cause my cousins and me to stand at attention. When she prayed, I felt that at any moment God was going to come out of a cloud or that Jesus was coming to rapture me home and I would not have time to repent for the sodas I had drunk and the candy I had eaten when I was not supposed to.

It was Grandmother Ella's passion and persistence in prayer that helped to shape my prayer life today. In the African American church, prayer has a unique sound. It contains a pleading and desperation like no other thing I have experienced. It starts with a humming, soon mixed with travailing, and a yearning that provokes and demands a response from heaven. Prayer has always been the root of our culture, dating back to slavery. For there was no greater prayer than the one for freedom. Slaves held on to the hope of freedom—whether on this side or in heaven, they knew that freedom was their right, and that one way or another, they would experience it.

FROM JAY

My friend Will Ford helped me understand why there is such a unique anointing for prayer with African Americans and why their prayers are such a key to seeing revival come to America. Will has been traveling around America since 2001 teaching on revival and prayer. And almost everywhere he goes, he carries a black kettle handed down to him by his ancestors. This black kettle was used by his great-great-grandmother Harriet Locket, a slave, for cooking and washing clothes. But it had an even greater use. Slaves were committed to prayer, even though it often resulted in severe beatings and punishment. They would plan secret prayer meetings to be held during the middle of the night, and "announce" it by singing songs in the field that day, songs like "Steal Away with Jesus." The slaves would gather for these secret prayer meetings, sometimes in "brush arbors" or "hush arbors," surrounded by trees and quilts that had been soaked in water and hung from the trees to muffle the sounds of prayer and singing. And often that black kettle would be turned upside down and propped a few inches off the ground on rocks. These slaves would then lay on the ground encircling the kettle with their mouths barely touching the rim, and as they would begin to fervently pray, their muffled prayers would be collected in the kettle, much like the prayers of the saints are collected in golden bowls in heaven (Revelation 5:8).[24]

I am somewhat overwhelmed when I think of the courage of these dear saints who risked so much to pray not just for their freedom, but for the freedom of our nation and for revival. When we mix our prayers with theirs, fire is added in heaven, according to Revelation 8, and at an appointed time these collected prayers set ablaze by the fire of God will be poured out on the earth to bring revival. The praying Church and praying people are the key to seeing racial unity and healing in our world.

---

24 Will Ford and Matt Lockett, *The Dream King: How the Dream of Martin Luther King, Jr Is Being Fulfilled to Heal Racism in America* (Newtype, 2018), 93-103.

In 2016, when I first took over as the campus pastor of our Greensboro location, I was wrestling with being a new pastor who was merging a historically black church with a predominantly white church. I had a million questions and very few answers. To make matters worse, I had no clue how to shift a culture that had been established for twenty years by leaders who were adored by the people I was now charged to lead. Bishop and Pastor Allen exuded servanthood and humility; they were two of the most humble people I had ever met. Our leadership styles were very different, but our hearts were the same. We both desired to see captives set free and the lost found.

One of the executive pastors from our Kannapolis campus told me something around that time that has helped me to this day. "It takes two or three years to change a culture," he said. "Whatever you desire to see happen in your campus begins when you decide to change the culture and become disciplined enough to stay the course despite the challenges ahead." This was not just about merging a people group or even different ethnicities. It was about embracing differences between cultures and welding them all together, while at the same time celebrating each one's own uniqueness. It was not easy. There are certain things that are staples of the black church that most white churches are often not even aware of, like the Negro National Anthem that was sung every Sunday morning at Henderson Grove Baptist church at the end of Sunday school, or the sound of a gospel choir singing songs with the lead singer hitting notes that it seemed not even some of the angels could hit. In the early days of the merger, I worried I had lost those things forever.

To shift any culture there has to be an admission that something is actually wrong with it. As Patrick Lencioni explains in his book

Five Dysfunctions of a Team: "A fractured team is just like a broken arm or leg: fixing it is always painful, and sometimes you have to rebreak it to make it heal correctly. And the re-break hurts more than the initial break, because you have to do it on purpose."[25] Could it be that God is breaking us to heal us? Maybe He is using this pivotal moment in history to usher us into revival. Maybe God is stripping away the stronghold of racism in our nation and building relationships that can change our future.

We all dream of opportunities to ensure that our families are secure and that we can live in the same communities and churches in a way that reflects heaven. And because God loves all His children equally, and we are all created in His image, we then have to ask ourselves, "Do I love all of His children equally?" God does not hold us responsible for the entire world. But He does hold us responsible for what He has given us to steward. Every influential person, black or white, must regularly ask themselves how they are utilizing the platform they have been given to help transform the lives of the people God has entrusted them to lead. If you are a business owner reading this book, I challenge you to honestly examine whether or not your team is diverse. If you are a pastor or a leader, does your church reflect heaven? When an application comes across your desk as an employer, manager, or supervisor, and you have the power to make the final decision, do you pick the most qualified person regardless of their ethnicity?

What are ways we can be proactive instead of reactive when situations arise that affect our world? Silence is loud and speaks volumes. I have been disappointed at times when Christian leaders say nothing. I have also felt deep conviction that I myself have not said enough. The next time you look at the company you work for, the church you are a part of, or even the world that you have created for yourself and your family, ask yourself this question: "Does this look like heaven?" My burden is to see the Church become the bride ready for Jesus' return. It has been awesome to see churches and

---

25 Patrick Lencioni, *The Five Dysfunctions of a Team* (San Francisco: Jossey-Bass, 2001), 37.

leaders across the nation begin the process of healing and taking ownership of injustices that have happened on our watch in our country. But it cannot stop there.

FROM JAY

In ancient days during the seventh month of each year, the Jewish people would make a pilgrimage to Jerusalem for the Feast of Tabernacles. If you have had the chance to visit Israel and Jerusalem, you know that this great and beautiful city is located on Mount Zion. The Scriptures often refer to "going up" to Jerusalem or "going up" to the Temple. As millions of Jews would ascend to the Holy City, they would sing the Songs of Ascent, which are Psalms 120–134. One of these songs, Psalm 133, contains just three verses that talk about unity. In verses 2-3 we read: "For harmony is as precious as the anointing oil that was poured over Aaron's head, that ran down his beard and onto the border of his robe. Harmony is as refreshing as the dew from Mount Hermon that falls on the mountains of Zion."

In these verses we find two images of unity: oil and mountain dew. Aaron was the high priest of Israel, and not just any oil could be poured over the head of the high priest. It required a special oil, a mix of olive oil, myrrh, cinnamon, cassia, and cane (Exodus 30). This oil was only used for anointing the priest and sacred objects in the Temple. The unity the psalmist is talking about is special, rare, not common, and cannot be found just anywhere. And this act of anointing Aaron connects us back to the previous psalm that talks about the coming Messiah, or the Anointed One. Aaron's anointing points us to the great High Priest, Jesus, the Head of the Church, who unifies us in worship in spite of diversity and difference so that we can accomplish His purposes. The oil flows down from the crown of Aaron's head, over his beard, across his collar, and eventually to the border of his robe. The robe is significant because the robe of the high priest contained the names of all twelve tribes of Israel. Oil represents the Holy Spirit. The beauty of this picture is that through the person of the Holy Spirit, regardless of what tribe we are from, what ethnicity, what age, what gender, or what denomination, we can be unified!

Then the psalmist talks about mountain dew. (I bet you didn't know David invented a soft drink!) Mount Hermon is located in northern Israel, along the Syrian border, and is Israel's highest mountain at over 9,000 feet elevation. It receives over sixty-three inches of rain and snow each year. Mount Zion, where Jerusalem sits, is only about 2,400 feet in elevation and is located in an arid and dry region, yet as you travel throughout this region and even further south towards the Dead Sea, you will see large plantations of fruit trees and flowers. This happens because of the "dew of Mt. Hermon" that flows from the northern part of the country all the way down to Mt. Zion and beyond.

What a beautiful picture of unity! It starts with the Holy Spirit who anoints the Head of the Church, Jesus. And then it flows down over His body, which is the Church, bringing life to dry and arid hearts, cities, and nations. When we are in unity with others, we become conduits for His anointing. But when we are in disunity, we block the flow of the Holy Spirit, restricting the life-giving flow from reaching others. Psalm 133 ends, "And there the LORD has pronounced his blessing, even life everlasting." Where? In the place where unity exists.

FROM DERRICK

My journey has led me to believe that the next frontier for the Church in America is a realization that racial reconciliation and unity is the heart of God. This is what He needs from us as individuals and what He needs from the Church: to be bold in calling out racism and systemic issues of oppression that keep the world in bondage. This is the counterculture and Kingdom culture that our churches need to embrace at this moment. Inequality is the Baal we must confront, just as Elijah confronted Baal on Mount Carmel. God doesn't need another Elijah; He needs you to be courageous and bold in your declaration of His truth and His goodness. That is how culture shifts.

Maybe you, too, have felt the whisperings of revival in your ears, or have felt the burden to speak out against injustice and racism. But maybe due to fear you have not done so. Remember: God will help you carry your burden when you stand in courage and boldness. Elijah shifted the culture with prayer, and so will we. That is the DNA of our people. The tears and desperation of our ancestors are the building blocks of the revival this nation desperately needs. They show us the way to the unity God so ardently desires from us. Prayer has always been a force that has shaped our country. What we need now is for the culture to shift again. It will take the sound of desperate people crying out to a loving Father who hears the cries of His children. The great revivals of old were nothing more than desperate people who gathered with no other motive but to see a move of God take place.

I don't want to be known as the generation that could have ended racism. I don't want to be the pastor who could have stood in the gap of racial division, but instead when God came looking, I was hiding or nowhere to be found, distracted by the news or cowering in fear because of cancel culture or because of a Philistine giant shouting threats of intimidation. Pastor Jay and I have decided to fill whatever gap of racial disunity the enemy desires to use to hinder revival. It's not enough to simply merge our churches and make our edifices more desirable. God is looking for faithful people to rebuild the wall of prayer and cry out for revival in our land. Prayer and intercession are the crucible for revival. Nothing can be welded without the fire of the Holy Spirit. There will always be challenges, things that desperately seek to divide us. Regardless of the leader of our country, the biases that we harbor in our hearts will be there. But I still believe that God can weld a nation together through His Spirit and cause the spirit of division among us to be completely destroyed by His love. It is His love that welds us, not our abilities.

FROM JAY

I believe we are positioned to see the greatest revival and the greatest outpouring of the Spirit of God ever in history, which will lead to one of the greatest harvests of souls we have ever seen. This, I believe, will be the blessing that God commands. The enemy is intent on keeping us divided in order to prevent this great revival and harvest. Derrick and I believe that what God has done in our lives and in our church is merely a peek into what He desires to do in other churches, among business leaders, in universities and schools, in cities, and all across our nation and world. And we, the sons of Issachar, modern day Zionists, last-days revivalists who are on the field in the fourth quarter, have an opportunity to do more than witness history.

We have the chance to MAKE history!

We believe every reader who has made it to the end of this book is feeling some weight and responsibility to steward the influence you have been given as it pertains to racial unity.

So, we invite you to turn the page and pray this prayer with us. It may be the end of *Welded*, but we believe it is the beginning of a great move of God!

PRAYER OF RECONCILIATION AND REPENTANCE

GOD,

We cry out in desperation for a world
that desperately needs You.

We cry out for the injustices that have plagued
our nation for centuries, and ask that heaven would
respond to our prayers for revival in our nation.

Father, we pray that You would forgive us for the
sin of racism in our nation and for any prejudices,
bitterness, or any thoughts we may still harbor
due to slavery and so many other injustices.

We pray that You would awaken America and the nations
of the world, and that You would unify us as Your bride.

Let us declare prophetic visions in the midst
of chaos, like Dr. King did when delivering
his great "I Have a Dream" speech.

Give us the courage and boldness the apostles
prayed for in Acts 4, courage we see demonstrated
in Rosa Parks, Billy Graham, and Harriet Tubman.

Raise up more deliverers, those with the spirit of a
modern-day Moses, who will confront the pharaohs
of our day and demand freedom for Your children.

Hear our cries, oh God, and respond to the disparities, economic barriers, and systemic racism that have affected black and brown communities for years.

Respond to the muffled prayers of the slaves who were beaten and died, having never tasted the freedoms that so many of us enjoy today!

Respond like You did in the days of the Azusa Street outpouring, when so many ethnicities gathered to cry out for a move of Your Spirit. Let our pleas be so united that You respond like You did on the Day of Pentecost.

We pray that You would raise up leaders in the White House and in Congress who would hear Your voice and follow Your lead.

We pray that churches and communities would become agents of change throughout the world. We incline our hearts and ears to heaven and patiently wait for You to speak, ready to obey and to respond with courage.

WELD US TOGETHER, WE PRAY!

In Jesus' Name, Amen.

ABOUT THE AUTHORS

DERRICK A. HAWKINS is a devoted husband to Roshonda Hawkins. Together, they pastor The Refuge Greensboro in Greensboro, NC. He is the loving father of five: Ronnette, Dashawn, Labrica, Adarion, Jaylen, and the late Derrick Jr. In the summer of 2016, Derrick Hawkins became the Senior Pastor of House of Refuge Deliverance Ministries. In that same year, he led House of Refuge Deliverance Ministries into the historic merger with The Refuge. Today, he continues to fearlessly lead the campus; bringing the vision to new places and fresh heights. Additionally, Derrick loves jogging, reading books, and adding to his shoe collection. He most enjoys quality time with his family, cooking and watching his sons play sports.

JAY STEWART grew up in Columbus, Georgia. He met his wife Melanie in high school, and they were married in 1983. Together with their five kids and grandkids, they live just outside of Charlotte, North Carolina. Jay is the Founding and Lead Pastor of The Refuge Church. In addition to leading The Refuge, he serves on several ministry boards, coaches pastors and church planters, and travels nationally and internationally to speak. He enjoys traveling, riding his Harley, playing basketball and golf, and spending time with his family.

ACKNOWLEDGMENTS

FROM DERRICK

With an abundance of gratitude, I would like to to acknowledge my children: Ronnette, DaShawn, Labrica, Adarion, Jaylen, and the late Derrick Jr. You motivate and inspire me to keep going in my toughest seasons/moments.

My parents Michael Bost (Gloria) and Melanie Kirkland. Thank you for always believing in me.

Honoring my grandmothers Betty McNeely, the late Ella Odessa Bost, and the late Anna Jean Jones. Great women of prayer and faith. These women have shaped my life and have helped me become the person I am today!

A special thanks to the late Kathy Lynn Robinson, who taught me the foundational kingdom principles and always displayed the unwavering love of Christ.
And to my Father-in-law, the late Ross Wilson.

The Refuge and The Refuge Greensboro. Bishop and Pastor Allen, who saw my potential and believed in me, not only trusting the voice of God but also entrusting me with their life's work. I'm forever grateful to them and their family for their countless sacrifices in helping to shape countless lives.

My good friend Lisa Whittle: thank you for encouraging me to write. You have been a tremendous inspiration.

To my new found relationships/friendships for which I am eternally grateful: David, Kobus, and the team at iDisciple Publishing, The Giving Company, and Dave Schroeder with WTA Media.

Jennie Puleo, you have been a godsend! Thanks so much for all of your support and patience in helping us deliver this message. I cannot thank you enough for all you have done. Love you much!

I stand on the shoulders of the generations before me who made preeminent sacrifices and paid the price for the freedoms that I have had the opportunity to experience today. Thanks so much for being a voice for the voiceless and the oppressed.

ACKNOWLEDGMENTS

FROM JAY

I want to first acknowledge my children: Haley, Yaya, Clay, Cole, and Caden. Next to marrying your mom, you guys (and my grandkids) are my greatest treasures on earth, and I am so proud of each of you.

I also want to send huge love and appreciation to the staff of The Refuge. This is not mine and Derrick's story, it is OUR story. Thank you for how you carry the Father's heart for unity. You are rock stars and a true dream team!

Massive hugs to Bishop William and Pastor Darlene Allen. Without your heart for the Kingdom and your willingness to surrender your dream to God, there would be no story.

My mom, Lynette Stewart, taught me and modeled for me what it means to love everyone, regardless of skin color or status. Your love is contagious!

I have to acknowledge my new friends David, Kobus, and the team at iDisciple Publishing and The Giving Company. You have been an answer to many prayers. Thank you for taking a chance! You will not regret it.

I am so thankful for our literary agent, Dave Schroeder with WTA Media. You will never know what it means that you believed in us and in our message.

Thanks to my assistant Jennie Puleo. What a blessing you are to us and to the Kingdom!

And to all of the courageous men and women from decades past who risked so much to see our nation take steps towards racial reconciliation, as well as those who continue to champion the vision, thank you for forging ahead. We are all beneficiaries.

CONNECTIONS

THE REFUGE CHURCH

 TheRefuge.net

JAY STEWART

 @PsJayStewart

 @PsJayStewart

 @PsJayStewart

DERRICK HAWKINS

 @derrickhwkns

 @derrickhwkns

 @derrickhwkns

IDISCIPLE PUBLISHING

 idisciplepublishing.com/welded

 @idisciplepublishingbookclub

NOTES

NOTES

NOTES

NOTES